DATE DUE			

Conrad Richter

Updated Edition

Twayne's United States Authors Series

Kenneth Eble, Editor

University of Utah

TUSAS 81

CONRAD RICHTER
(1890–1968).
Courtesy of Alfred A. Knopf, Inc.

Conrad Richter

Updated Edition

Edwin W. Gaston, Jr.

Emeritus, Stephen F. Austin State University

Twayne Publishers
A Division of G.K. Hall & Co. • Boston

Conrad Richter, Updated Edition

Edwin W. Gaston, Jr.

Copyright 1989 by G.K. Hall & Co.
All rights reserved.
Published by Twayne Publishers
A Division of G.K. Hall & Co.
70 Lincoln Street
Boston, Massachusetts 02111

Copyediting supervised by Barbara Sutton
Book production by Patricia D'Agostino
Book design by Barbara Anderson

Typeset in 11 pt. Garamond
by Williams Press Inc., Albany, New York

Printed on permanent/durable acid-free paper
and bound in the United States of America

Library of Congress Cataloging-in-Publication Data

Gaston, Edwin W.
    Conrad Richter / Edwin W. Gaston, Jr.—Updated ed.
       p. cm.—(Twayne's United States authors series : TUSAS 81)
    Bibliography: p. 140
    Includes index.
    ISBN 0-8057-7530-7 (alk. paper)
    1. Richter, Conrad, 1890-1968—Criticism and interpretation.
I. Title. II. Series.
PS3535.I429Z68   1989
813'.52—dc19

Contents

About the Author

A native of Nacogdoches, Texas, to which his great-great-grandfather immigrated during the time of the early nineteenth century Republic, Edwin W. Gaston, Jr., can empathize with Conrad Richter's devotion to the southwestern United States. The region, in fact, has influenced his writing as much as it did Richter's. Gaston's first book-length publication was the literary history *The Early Novel of the Southwest* (1960). His original edition of *Conrad Richter* followed in 1965, and his analytical study *Eugene Manlove Rhodes: Cowboy Chronicler,* in 1967. Gaston coedited *Southwestern American Literature: A Bibliography* (1980) and contributed essays to *A Bibliographical Guide to Midwestern Literature* (1981), *Dictionary of Literary Biography* (1981), *Fifty Western Writers* (1982), and *Dictionary of American Biography* (1988). His essays and reviews have been published in such journals as the *New Mexico Quarterly, Publications of the Texas Folklore Society, Southwestern American Literature,* and *Western American Literature.*

Gaston retired in 1986 and was named professor emeritus of English at Stephen F. Austin State University, where he also served as chairman of English and journalism, graduate dean, and academic vice-president. He also taught at Texas Tech University and, under a Fulbright grant, at the University of Helsinki and the Swedish School of Economics in Helsinki. Before entering teaching, Gaston edited and published magazines and newspapers and engaged in radio broadcasting. He holds bachelor's and master's degrees from Stephen F. Austin State University and a doctorate from Texas Tech University.

For twelve years, Gaston served as national president of the Alpha Chi national honor society. He also has been an officer in numerous regional and national professional societies. His present memberships include the Modern Language Association and its south-central affiliate, Southwestern American Literature Association, Texas Folklore Society, and Western American Literature Association.

Gaston and his wife, Martha, have three sons and four grandchildren.

Preface

In 1965, when *Conrad Richter* was published as the eighty-first volume in this series, Richter was vigorous at seventy-five years of age and still writing regularly. He added two novels and a novelette to the corpus of his published works and received additional accolades before his death in 1968. Ten years after his death, a third collection of his stories, previously published individually, was issued.

That is to say that events transpiring in the almost quarter-century since the publication of *Conrad Richter*, being updated here, understandably have altered some of my perceptions. Mainly, I now believe, as I did not originally, that scholars recognize that Richter's best works properly belong among the foremost historical novels and stories in American letters. In addition to my book, its subsequent Portuguese language edition published in Brazil, and my three anthologized bibliographical and analytical essays, three books and numerous essays by other scholars have contributed to the establishment of Richter's enhanced literary reputation. Moreover, the 1979 televising of *The Awakening Land* (originally the Pennsylvania-Ohio historical trilogy *The Trees, The Fields,* and *The Town*) has brought Richter much greater popular recognition than his book sales and the earlier films of three of his novels. Although still not a household name, Conrad Richter clearly has emerged posthumously from the obscurity that he himself encouraged during his lifetime in the interest of his art and of his personal and familial privacy.

Given the present scholarly and popular acceptance of Richter's works, I no longer feel the compulsion here that I did in my original prefatory statement to chasten scholars for Richter's neglect, typified by the reaction to the selection of Richter's autobiographical novel *The Waters of Kronos* for the 1960 National Book Award for fiction. Nevertheless, because the award served as a turning point in Richter's recognition, I should recall the circumstances of the competition. In preaward speculation, Harper Lee's *To Kill A Mockingbird,* John Updike's *Rabbit, Run,* and John Hersey's *The Child Buyer* all justifiably had been mentioned prominently; but, despite good reviews, Richter's novel had not. Numerous scholars, therefore, were unprepared for the outcome when the award to Richter was announced. What they had failed to take into consideration was, first, the artistry represented by *The Waters of Kronos* and, second, that for nearly half a century Richter had been publishing accomplished novels and stories, several of which already had been highly honored. For example, Richter's *The Town* had received the 1951 Pulitzer Prize for fiction; and *The Sea of Grass,* his first novel, and *The Trees* together had earned Richter the 1942 gold medal for fiction awarded by the Society of Libraries of New York University.

But if time has altered my earlier perception about the scholarly and popular neglect of Richter's work, it has not changed other main ideas I originally articulated about his life and work. One of those concerned Richter's use of personal experience for characters and plots to the extent that he is one of America's most autobiographical creative writers. His fiction derives not only from his own life, but from the lives of numerous relatives and others he knew or learned about through painstaking research. Those autobiographical impulses and the fact that no full-scale biography of Richter had been written prompted me in my original book, as it does here, to devote substantial attention to biographical detail. My sources for such material included Conrad Richter himself, his literary agent Paul R. Reynolds, Jr., and Richter's New Mexico friend Professor T. M. Pearce.

Another idea I stressed originally and reiterate here is that Richter's autobiographical impulses naturally influence his literary themes. Himself a reticent person, who devoted his life to plain living and high thinking, Richter celebrates simple goodness reflected in quiet courage, dedication, individualism, and persistence. Those were recurrent qualities he found in the lives of pioneers who he believed had made this nation great— qualities, as he further believed, too often absent in modern life. Richter's heroes and heroines acquire admirable self-discipline and character improvement as a result of hardship and suffering. His failures usually fall because of ease and luxury. Such thematic preferences link Richter and Faulkner, who also celebrates "courage and honor and hope and pride and compassion and pity and sacrifice" that have been the "glory" of the human past.

Still another point I stressed in my first Richter book and underscore here is that Richter works from an identifiably philosophical base. That base consists of quasi-scientific ideas through which Richter seeks to reconcile mind and matter, science and religion (physics and metaphysics). In the main, Richter's philosophy would be more acceptable were it expressed more by analogy than by stated proposition and particularly had he refrained from borrowing scientific terminology and using it in a sense science does not recognize. Nevertheless, as Richter insisted, the philosophy serves as the *"overtones"* of his novels and stories (inferentially, the *undertones*). Recognition of it is essential to a complete understanding of character, plot, and theme in his work. Furthermore, in being cognizant of Richter's philosophy, the reader can be all the more appreciative of the author's artistic virtuosity that allows him to achieve a higher level of truth in the stories and novels than in the essays.

Finally, here as in my original work, I emphasize that Richter's writing reflects clarity, economy, and fidelity to colloquial expression. His ability to telescope event and space and time enables him to achieve even in his brief passages the evocation of literal and abstract (including mystical and mythical) levels of awareness. His accomplished simplicity of style thus complements his thematic celebration of uncomplicated virtue. It also enables him to avoid the pitfalls of didacticism and sentimentality that might ordinarily be expected to accompany such themes.

In the preparation of the original edition of *Conrad Richter,* I was the fortunate recipient of unstinting assistance from many persons and institutions. To those persons still living, to the memories of the others, and to the institutions, I herewith express my continuing appreciation. Particularly, I reiterate my gratitude to the late Conrad and Harvena Achenbach Richter and to Richter's literary agent, the late Paul R. Reynolds, Jr., for granting me interviews and for allowing me to inspect their relevant notebooks and papers.

For this updated edition of *Conrad Richter* I have again received assistance from some of those original supporters and also from new ones. Foremost among the carryover supporters is my wife, Martha Middlebrook Gaston, herself a keen student of Richter's works. Among my new supporters are our grandchildren, whom I feel obliged to mention not only out of grandfatherly pride but also out of gratitude for the younger ones's refraining from distracting me at work and from rearranging my home study and notes when I was out of the house. More professional but no less considerate assistance from new supporters has come also from the special collections librarians at Stephen F. Austin State University, Linda Nicklas and Pamela Lynn Palmer; Betsy Williams, of Alfred A. Knopf, Inc.; and from the following members of the Twayne United States Authors Series editorial staff: Kenneth Eble, general editor; Elizabeth B. Kubik, editor-in-chief; Athenaide Dallett, editor; Barbara Sutton, manuscript editor; the copy editor Josephine Donovan; Liz Traynor, associate editor; Rosalie Fitzgerald, administrative assistant; Barbara Anderson, art director; and Patricia D'Agostino, production assistant. I salute them one and all.

Edwin W. Gaston, Jr.

Nacogdoches, Texas

Chronology

1890	Conrad Richter born 13 October in Pine Grove, Pennsylvania, first of three sons of John Absalom and Charlotte Esther Henry Richter.
1899	Family moves to Selinsgrove, Pennsylvania.
1906	Graduates from Tremont, Pennsylvania, high school.
1906–1913	Works variously as a teamster, farm laborer, bank clerk, timberman, subscription salesman, newspaper reporter and editor, and private secretary in Pennsylvania and Ohio.
1913	"How Tuck Went Home," first story.
1914–1915	"Brothers of No Kin," first widely acclaimed story published first in 1914 and republished in 1915.
1915	Marries Harvena Achenbach, of Pine Grove, 24 March.
1917	Harvena, only child, born 13 March.
1922–1928	Resides on a farm in Clarks Valley, Pennsylvania, engaging in writing fiction and in publishing.
1924	*Brothers of No Kin and Other Stories.* Charlotte Richter dies 8 October.
1926	*Human Vibration,* first book-length philosophical essay.
1927	*Principles in Bio-Physics.*
1928	Family moves to Albuquerque, New Mexico.
1936	*Early Americana.*
1937	*The Sea of Grass.*
1940	*The Trees.* John Absalom Richter dies 17 January.
1942	*Tacey Cromwell.* Receives gold medal for literature by the Society of Libraries of New York University for *The Sea of Grass* and *The Trees.*
1943	*The Free Man.*
1944	Receives honorary Doctor of Letters degree from Susquehanna University.
1946	*The Fields.* Receives award of merit from the Pennsylvania German Society.

1947   *Always Young and Fair*. Receives Ohioana Library medal
          award for literature.

1950   Family moves from Albuquerque to Pine Grove. *The
          Town*.

1951   Awarded the Pulitzer Prize for fiction.

1953   *The Light in the Forest*.

1955   *The Mountain on the Desert*.

1957   *The Lady*.

1958   Receives honorary Doctor of Letters degree from the
          University of New Mexico.

1960   *The Waters of Kronos*. Granted National Book award for
          fiction.

1962   *A Simple Honorable Man*.

1964   *The Grandfathers*.

1966   *A Country of Strangers*. Receives honorary Doctor of
          Philosophy degree from Temple University, honorary Doc-
          tor of Letters degree from Lafayette College, and honorary
          Doctor of Humane Letters degree from Lebanon Valley
          College.

1967   *Over the Blue Mountain*.

1968   *The Aristocrat*. Dies 30 October.

1972   Harvena Achenback Richter dies 7 March.

1978   *The Rawhide Knot and Other Stories*.

1988   *Writing to Survive: The Private Notebooks of Conrad
          Richter*.

Chapter One
The Spirit of Place

Attention has been called frequently to similarities between Conrad Richter and Willa Cather, Elizabeth Madox Roberts, or even A. B. Guthrie, Jr. But if criticism has correctly pointed out the common interests of these novelists in pioneer character types and historical subjects, it has failed to note certain obvious parallels between Richter and Thomas Wolfe. The latter comparison, although somewhat academic, proves useful in emphasizing two factors in Richter's life that have conspicuously influenced his writing. Both Richter and Wolfe are heavily indebted to family and to home, or, more particularly in the case of Richter, to what Mary Austin called the "spirit of place." Like Wolfe's, Richter's family tradition extends into early Pennsylvania and provides him with an extraordinary incidence of character, plot, and setting. And each writer, in the use of such appropriated personal materials, either has expressed or implied an alienation from at least some segment of the family circle.

But here the similarity ends. Wolfe's father moved from Pennsylvania to North Carolina, but Richter's remained on native soil. Only the author himself, in fact, broke the family residential permanence—and that only temporarily, but significantly in its effect upon his literary career—with a sojourn in the Southwest. Moreover, Richter's family connection with the Lutheran ministry, which helped turn his works more often than is generally recognized toward the mystical and mythical, has no direct parallel in Wolfe. Finally, if Wolfe could not go home again—could not, that is, completely bridge the gulf of familial alienation—Richter, if he did break in any other than a subconscious way, effected such a reconciliation in his final works.

Family Roots

The Richter family itself, by comparison with the author's maternal lineage, reached America belatedly in the middle of the nineteenth century. Its first arrival, J. Michael Richter (1834–1915), Conrad's

1

grandfather, emigrated at the age of eighteen from Germany to Reading, Pennsylvania. An uncle living in San Antonio, Texas, had wanted the youth to come to the Southwest. But being without funds, J. Michael Richter wrote wryly, "Send me a cane so that I can walk." Whether or not a cane ever arrived is not recorded in the Richter family annals. That J. Michael remained in Pennsylvania, however, has been taken by his heirs to mean that more financially tangible means of transportation did not come from Texas.

For a livelihood, J. Michael Richter served as a section foreman and later as a tie inspector for a railroad. His occupation doubtless contributed to the interest in railroads that his grandson Conrad Richter manifests in such fictional pieces as "Swanson's 'Home Sweet Home,' " "The Head of His House," "Smoke over the Prairie," and *The Town*.[1]

J. Michael Richter married Susannah Michael (1834–96), a woman of German and Welsh descent from whom her grandson Conrad derived his middle given name. The couple's son, John Absalom Richter, Conrad's father, was born 11 September 1861 in Reading.

As shown in his son's novels, *The Waters of Kronos* and *A Simple Honorable Man* (in both of which he is portrayed as Harry Donner), John Richter operated a general store in Pine Grove, Pennsylvania, and sold tobacco on the road until, in middle age, he decided to prepare for the Lutheran ministry. On 4 September 1884 he married Charlotte Esther Henry, of Pine Grove, whose family residence in America dated to the early eighteenth century or to about one hundred years before that of the Richter family.

To his mother's family, much more so than to his father's, Conrad Richter is indebted for fictional materials. The following table shows the extent of his indebtedness.[2]

Person	Relationship to Conrad Richter	Fictional Service
Henry Conrad	Great-great-great-grandfather	In part the model for Henry Free in *The Free Man*
Frederick Conrad (Son to Henry)	Great-great-grandfather	In part the model for Henry Free in *The Free Man*
Henry W. Conrad (Son to Frederick)	Great-grandfather	General source, but less discernible than others

Sarah Ann Conrad (Daughter to Henry W.)	Grandmother	Mary Scarlett Morgan, first wife of Elijah Morgan, in *The Waters of Kronos* and in *A Simple Honorable Man*
Elias Strickhouser Henry	Grandfather	Elijah Morgan in *The Waters of Kronos* and in *A Simple Honorable Man*
Frederick William Conrad	Great-uncle	Uncle Timothy in *The Waters of Kronos* and in *A Simple Honorable Man*
Victor Lafayette Conrad (Brother to Sarah Ann)	Great-uncle	Uncle Howard in *The Waters of Kronos* and in *A Simple Honorable Man*
Charlotte Esther Henry (Daughter to Sarah Ann and Elias Henry)	Mother	Valeria Donner in *The Waters of Kronos* and in *A Simple Honorable Man*
George Conrad Henry (Brother to Charlotte)	Uncle	Peter Morgan in *The Waters of Kronos* and in *A Simple Honorable Man*

The first in Conrad Richter's maternal family to come to America, Henry Conrad (ca. 1727–?) arrived in 1749 in Philadelphia and settled in Montgomery County, Pennsylvania. In his great-great-great-grandson Conrad Richter's novel, *The Free Man,* the character Henry Free also landed at Philadelphia and subsequently moved inland; but Henry Free came from Germany. According to a family account, Henry Conrad came to this country to escape the persecution of the Protestant Huguenots in eastern France.

Henry Conrad's son, Frederick Conrad (1759–1827), lived in Worcester near Norristown, Pennsylvania, and served as a squire, state legislator, and Congressman—offices held by Henry Free in *The Free Man.* A blacksmith by trade, as well as a part-time teacher in a singing school, Frederick Conrad owed his congressional elections in 1802 and 1804 to the agrarian Jeffersonian Republicans. His affiliation with agrarianism is a link to similar sympathies that his great-great-grandson Conrad Richter displays in essays and fiction.

Frederick's son, Henry W. Conrad (1789–1841) became a major in the War of 1812, a state legislator, and the first of his family to reside in Pine Grove. There he built the Mansion House tavern and also operated a general store. Elected a magistrate, Henry W. Conrad punished "sinners" who said "damn" on Sunday. But his basic humanity was reflected in his sheltering of runaway Negro slaves, one of whom, Black Hetty, lived long enough to nurse his great-grandson Conrad Richter. Black Hetty also inspired a character of the same name in *The Sea of Grass*.

Henry Conrad's wife, Elizabeth Kendall (1791–1852), introduced an English strain into Conrad Richter's bloodlines. More important to the shaping of her great-grandson's literary career, however, her children brought by professional choice and marriage a family association with the Lutheran ministry. Henry and Elizabeth Kendall Conrad's daughter, Sarah Ann (1822–69), married the Reverend Elias Strickhouser Henry (1823–97). Henry's ministry made him the model for the Reverend Elijah Morgan in *The Waters of Kronos* and *A Simple Honorable Man*. From 1852 to 1897, the total length of his ministry, Elias Henry was minister of St. John's Church, organized in 1845 in Pine Grove.

In fiction, Conrad Richter emphasizes the spartan qualities both of Elias Henry and of J. Michael Richter, his other grandfather. In life, both men, as Richter pointed out in a published reminiscence, maintained such demeanors that their grandchildren came into their presence with awe and hesitation.[3] Even the author's father and mother felt highly honored by a mere visit from her father, a man nevertheless described by his grandson Conrad as having a dry sense of humor and commanding such respect from his parishioners that mourners overflowed two adjacent churches required for his funeral. Of his grandfather Richter, Conrad recalled his astonishment that the elder once served the youth a glass of water. Little wonder then that, when he created fictional characters modeled on his grandfathers, Conrad Richter attributed to them restraint bordering on aloofness but tempered in such a manner as to evoke affectionate respect.

Sarah Ann Conrad Henry's brother, the Reverend Frederick William Conrad (1816–98), likewise held Lutheran pastorates at St. John's in Hagerstown, at the First Church in Dayton, at the Trinity in Lancaster, and at the Messiah in Philadelphia. Additionally, from 1862 to 1898, he edited the *Lutheran Observer*. That publication is called the *Lutheran Messenger* in Conrad Richter's novels *The Waters of Kronos* and *A Simple Honorable Man*.

Another of Sarah Ann's brothers, the Reverend Victor Lafayette Conrad (1824–1900), was a professor at Gettysburg College and, for thirty years, also an editor of the *Observer*. Sarah Ann Conrad and Elias Henry's son, the Reverend George Conrad Henry (1856–1909), was a Lutheran minister at St. John's in Des Moines and at Memorial in Shippensburg, Pennsylvania.

Sarah Ann Conrad Henry died 12 August 1869 from injuries sustained in an accidental fall. Ten years earlier, on 22 April 1859, she had borne a daughter, Charlotte Esther Henry, who became Conrad Richter's mother. From his mother, much more than from his father, Richter derived deep sensitivity and, as he stressed in a radio broadcast, his proclivity for writing.[4] For that reason, Richter also suggested, he felt a spiritual kinship with the British writer W. H. Hudson, whose depiction of his mother reminded Richter of his own.

John Richter's decision in middle age to enter the ministry had a temporarily unsettling effect upon his family. The nature of the confusion can be imagined from Conrad Richter's description of a similar experience by a fictional character (Harry Donner) in the novel *A Simple Honorable Man*.[5] In that story, a child contrasts the strength his father had demonstrated in his grocery store and with his "soaring bass voice" in the church choir with the spent condition his father appeared to be in after reaching his agonizing decision to start life anew as a minister. The father in that moment impresses the child as someone he "hardly knew."

Inherent in that fictional account of his father's ministerial "call" is not only the real-life confusion Richter felt consciously, but the resentment he experienced at least subconsciously. An explicit statement of such resentment is made by Richter in an article, which recalls the "long and sometimes terrible prayers" he had to endure—prayers "almost unintelligible, filled with groans."[6]

In his fiction Richter demonstrated conscious doubts about—indeed, subconscious alienation from—his earthly father and his Spiritual. And the result is a mystical quest by his fictional characters for reconciliation with both, an achievement imperfectly realized. The theme of the search for the Spiritual Father (for whom the earthly is a symbol), of course, is common to fiction. In part it grew naturally out of the materials with which Richter worked. The effect of personal experience on this thematic preference, however, must not be underestimated.

Before he decided to enter the ministry, John Richter and his wife had had all of their children, three sons: Conrad, the fictional John Donner of *The Waters of Kronos* and *A Simple Honorable Man,* born in 1890; Joseph, the fictional Gene Donner, in 1893; and Frederick, the fictional Tim Donner, in 1894. To the sons, as the eldest recalls, their father was "not so severe" as their grandfathers; but he was still distant to his own: "He could be very entertaining and jovial, especially to visitors and other children than his own. A kind of manly reserve remained between him and his sons," none of whom had "his vitality and vigor."[7] This "manly reserve" further separated John Richter from his son Conrad, although it did so subconsciously more nearly than consciously for the boy. No evidence suggests an open break between the father and the eldest offspring, however.

His father's "vigor," Conrad Richter further notes, was evident to others, sometimes even in ways surprising to the author. An elderly coal miner once "told me," Conrad Richter said, "he had read *The Sea of Grass.* "That colonel in there,' he said, 'didn't you have your father in mind when you wrote it?' I was a little startled."[8] More pertinent to Conrad Richter's thinking, however, is not the misconception of others, but the element of "vigor" itself. This quality Richter feels to be typical of men and women of the past but one too frequently missing in those of today. The concept of "vigor" underlies his theories of life as expressed in such philosophical essays as *Human Vibration,* and it appears repeatedly in his fiction.

Enrolled at the age of thirty-eight in 1899 at Susquehanna College, John Richter was something of an anachronism among his younger ministerial classmates. Nevertheless, he enjoyed the camaraderie and delighted in the intellectual stimulation. His immersion in study, however, sometimes provided his family with unintended humorous diversion. In *A Simple Honorable Man,* therefore, Conrad Richter points out that the protagonist's (Harry Donner's) mealtime consists of Greek and Hebrew studied "with fried potatoes and mush" for breakfast; logic and philosophy considered with "ham and eggs for midday dinner"; and Latin quotations, not to mention scholarly discussions with a college friend or two "along with mush and milk for supper."[9]

Formally ordained in 1904, John Richter and his family set out for the first of his seven parishes. In *A Simple Honorable Man,* Harry Donner serves only three; and, in fact, at one stage in the writing of the novel, Conrad Richter considered restricting the number to one. But in real life, John Richter served seven, establishing at the first what was to become the pattern of his ministry. "If anybody had tried to make a list of 'outstanding Lutheran pastors in Pennsylvania in the 1930's," wrote a recent church historian, "John Richter's name would probably have been overlooked. His genius was in his obscure ministry to simple people. He never got an honorary degree."[10]

The minister's wife, Charlotte Henry Richter, died 8 October 1924 in Allentown and was buried at Pine Grove. Meanwhile, the three sons—Conrad, Joe, and Fred—had grown to manhood. The details of Conrad Richter's life will be presented below. Fred Richter became a businessman, working as a buyer and credit manager for a China works in Syracuse, New York. Joe Richter engaged in a career as a civil engineer in Reading, Pennsylvania.

Thus, with his wife's death and the earlier departure of their sons to professional pursuits, John Richter in 1926 accepted a second "call" to the Scalp Level parish, where he remained much of the time until his retirement at the age of seventy-two in 1933. But even after retirement, the old minister, as in his son's novel *A Simple Honorable Man,* remained active. Part of the time, he lived with Dr. and Mrs. George Nicely, the regular minister and his wife, in the parsonage of First Church in Johnstown, Pennsylvania, and helped with the parish visiting and preaching. Each of his sons had offered their father a retirement home with them, but John Richter prefered to be in a setting that allowed him to be as active as possible.[11] He died 17 January 1940 and was buried beside his wife at Pine Grove.

The Making of A Writer

Conrad Michael Richter was born 13 October 1890 in Pine Grove. Although a quiet youth, he early evidenced the same quality that he pinpointed in his father, whom he described as "restless." To satisfy this wanderlust, Conrad ravished Harry Castlemon's boys books as a vicarious substitute for an earlier misadventure. At the age of six Richter and his cousin Henry W. Irwin, aged eight, failed in an attempt to run away to the "Wild West."[12] The plot aborted as the result of a betrayal by Henry's sister Beth, who hated to think of her brother and cousin being tortured by Sioux Indians. If their earlier plans failed, however, the boys' efforts to go west ultimately materialized. Richter, as a young man, investigated a silver and lead mining venture in the

Coeur d'Alene region of Idaho; and, as an older man, he resided for a number of years in Albuquerque. Irwin eventually went to Montana. Concerning his lifelong love for books and reading, Richter recalled in a radio broadcast that he was the type of reader who could completely immerse himself in the book at hand. If someone spoke to him, he said, he might not hear; and, even if the speaker succeeded in getting Richter's attention, Richter kept his mind mostly on the book all the while he listened. Then, as Richter further explained, once he had completed reading a book by a given author he would search immediately for another book by the same writer. "Often," however, Richter said that he had "been disappointed in the second book of an author." But sometimes, under the author's "unseen hand" Richter would find himself in as "great a transport of delight" as he had been in while reading the first book by that writer.[13]

When Richter was nine, his father's decision to prepare for the ministry at Susquehanna College removed the family from Pine Grove to Selinsgrove. There Conrad attended Susquehanna Preparatory School. In 1906, he completed his high school education at Tremont, Pennsylvania, his father's first parish.

Although his parents had hoped he would prepare for the ministry himself, Richter turned to a series of odd jobs. First he worked as a teamster, and then he secured employment at the Westinghouse Machine Company in East Pittsburgh, an experience that furnished him with materials for such short stories as "The Old Debt" in which the principal character, also a minister's son, works for the same concern. But, developing a distaste for industrial work, Richter soon became in turn a farm laborer, a bank clerk, a timberman, and a subscription salesman— occupations that also figured prominently in his fiction.[14]

In 1910, when he was twenty years old, Richter chanced upon a series of ten articles on the American newspaper that the *Bookman* had published in 1904. He determined immediately to become a journalist. In fact, on the same day that he completed reading the articles, Richter applied for and secured a reporter's job on the Johnstown (Pennsylvania) *Journal*. He had not had much experience as a writer even though, while a bank clerk, he regularly sent "squibs" to the Philadelphia newspapers. Moreover, as he recalled, writing was not easy for him. "As a boy in school," he said, "writing went extremely hard."[15] Nevertheless, once he became a journalist, Richter experienced pleasure in feeling "words flow on a typewriter" and then seeing them in print. The same type of pleasure in composition, he added, caused him to write his first fictional stories.

On the Johnstown *Journal,* the pay was not particularly encouraging, but the praise Richter elicited from a hard-bitten city editor—"Boy, you'll go far"—whetted his enthusiasm. That his newspaper experience proved profitable in other ways can be seen in Richter's polished style, which he, like Hemingway, attributed largely to journalism.

From Johnstown, Richter graduated to jobs on the Patton *Courier,* which he edited; the Pittsburgh *Dispatch;* and the Johnstown *Leader.* Then Richter worked for two years as a private secretary in Cleveland, Ohio. There, on 6 September 1913, he published his first work of fiction, the short story "How Tuck Went Home," in *Cavalier,* a Munsey publication edited by Robert Hobart Davis.

In April, 1914, Richter published a second story, "Brothers of No Kin," in the *Forum.* It had a remarkable reception, being chosen by E. J. O'Brien[16] as the best story of the year and being reprinted in the 4 June 1915 issue of *Reedy's Mirror* and in the 26 September 1915 issue of *Illustrated Sunday Magazine.* Editors suddenly began soliciting more of Richter's work. "It was the sort of opportunity no youth today would fail to grasp," Richter said, "but I was too young, and callow and too stubborn."[17]

This stubborn refusal to respond to editorial solicitation actually represented disillusionment with the financial rewards for publishing. Only after mustering his courage and asking for payment from the *Forum* for "Brothers of No Kin" did Richter receive a paltry twenty-five dollars. "I had just been married, had sober obligations, and told myself stubbornly that if this was what one got for the 'best' story of the year," Richter said, "I had better stick to business and write in my spare time only the type of story that would fetch a fair price."[18]

Richter had been married 24 March 1915 to Harvena Achenbach. Like her husband a native of Pine Grove, where she was born 12 January 1896 Mrs. Richter was six years her husband's junior and, therefore, had not been, as is sometimes assumed, his childhood sweetheart. In fact, the couple did not meet until 1914 when Richter visited relatives in Pine Grove, where her father, Gregory Achenbach, was a baker, teacher, and squire for forty years.

Conrad and Harvena Achenbach Richter had one child, a daughter Harvena, born 13 March 1917. After taking an undergraduate degree from the University of New Mexico and a master's degree from New York University, the daughter followed in her father's literary footsteps. Her stories and poems have appeared in the *New Yorker*, the *Saturday Evening Post*, and other publications. She resides in Albuquerque, New Mexico.

Turning to what he hoped would "fetch a fair price," Richter began doing stories for *John Martin's Book*. His serial, in fact, was the first published by this children's monthly magazine. Later, in Reading, Richter published for about a year his own *Junior Magazine*, doing the writing, as well as the editing and the advertising sales and copywriting, and using a dozen pen names. The *Junior Magazine* discontinued publication during World War I, but Richter himself continued in the publishing business, first in Reading and then, until 1928, in Harrisburg. Meanwhile, short stories by Richter had appeared regularly in *Outlook, Ladies' Home Journal*, the *Saturday Evening Post, American*, and *Every Week*. And twelve of the pieces the author had drawn into his first collected volume, *Brothers of No Kin and Other Stories* (1924).

Simultaneously, Richter was undergoing a process of self-education. Beginning about 1913 and continuing as recently as 1955, he investigated the philosophical problems of life in its entirety. The initial result was a book-length essay, *Human Vibration* (1925). It was followed by the shorter companion work, *Principles in Bio-Physics (1927)*, a paperback, and then by the most ambitious of the three, *The Mountain on the Desert* (1955).

In 1928, the critical illness that almost claimed the life of his wife forced Richter to sell his business and farm in the East and to move to Albuquerque, New Mexico. The abrupt change of residence was made with less difficulty than might be imagined, however, because of a factor Richter explained years afterward in discussing W. H. Hudson's *Far Away and Long Ago:* "So keenly was I as a reader interested in his [Hudson's] obscure Spanish-speaking neighbors and so intimately was I made acquainted with them that years later when I took my small family to New Mexico to live I found the Spanish-speaking people there familiar to me as old acquaintances, all curiously due to my introductions to their cousins in a distant land and age."[19] In New Mexico the Richters remained—save for winters spent in Arizona, California, and Texas and for a few summers in Pennsylvania—until 1950. In that year Richter and his wife acquired a house in their native Pine Grove and returned to permanent residence, save for winters spent in Bradenton, Florida.

The enforced move to the Southwest proved fortunate for Richter's literary career. It brought about a searching reexamination of his purposes and led to the decision to write "the best stories" of which he was capable. Nine of these stories—previously published in such magazines as *Ladies' Home Journal* and the *Saturday Evening Post*—Richter collected as *Early Americana* (1936), his first volume of southwestern fiction. Some of those stories were collected again and augmented with still other short fictional pieces, previously published individually, in the volume *The Rawhide Knot and Other Stories,* issued in 1978, ten years after Richter's death. The publication of *Early Americana* marked the permanent affiliation of Richter with the publishing house of Alfred A. Knopf and with the literary agents Paul R. Reynolds, Sr., and, later, Paul R. Reynolds, Jr.

Richter capitalized upon the success of his stories set in his newly adopted region by writing four southwestern novels: *The Sea of Grass* (1937), his first full-length work of fiction; *Tacey Cromwell* (1942); *The Mountain on the Desert* (1955); and *The Lady* (1957). The last two, however, were published after Richter had returned to permanent residence in Pennsylvania. Both *The Sea of Grass* and *Tacey Cromwell* were adapted for motion pictures, the first two of Richter's six novels to be filmed.

During his residence in the Southwest, Richter also conceived and wrote his monumental Pennsylvania-Ohio trilogy of novels, *The Trees* (1940), *The Fields* (1946), and *The Town* (1950). *The Town* won the 1951 Pulitzer Prize for fiction. Earlier, in 1942, Richter had received the gold medal for literature from the Society of Libraries of New York University. The award was for *The Sea of Grass* and *The Trees,* the latter of which, chosen as a Book-of-the-Month Club selection for March 1940, had become Richter's best-selling novel. Then, in 1947, Richter received the Ohioana Library medal for *The Trees* and *The Fields.* Still other honors he received were honorary doctorates from Susquehanna University (1944), the University of New Mexico (1958), and Temple University, Lafayette College, and Lebanon Valley College (all 1966).

During the period of his residence in New Mexico, *The Trees* marked Richter's first significant deviation from the use of his adopted Southwest as the background for fiction. But he never quite abandoned his native East as the source of fictional materials. Indeed, during the nearly six years from 1928 until 1934, while he was tediously collecting new materials, he had relied for a living on the type of popular story he had begun writing in 1914 in Pennsylvania. Among these stories was

"The King Was in the Kitchen," published in the May 1932 issue of *Woman's Home Companion*. It antedated by two years Richter's first noteworthy Western story, "Early Marriage," published first in the 7 April 1934 issue of the *Saturday Evening Post* and later in *Early Americana*.

While still residing in New Mexico, Richter interlaced among his southwestern stories and novels and his eastern trilogy two lesser novels and several stories set outside the Southwest. *The Free Man*, an American Revolutionary War novel, was published in 1943; and *Always Young and Fair*, a novel concerned in part with the Spanish-American War, in 1947. Among the stories, "Good Neighbors" was published in the 30 October 1943 issue of the *Saturday Evening Post*.

Between the publication of *The Sea of Grass* and *The Trees*, Richter worked irregularly as a writer for Metro-Goldwyn-Mayer motion picture studios in Hollywood. "I was not there steadily but in the manner of studios with most authors," he said, "that is, a session of three or four months annually."[20] The experience, however, proved disillusioning and prompted Richter to turn his full attention to the historical trilogy and other writing efforts.

Returning in 1950 to permanent residence in Pine Grove, Richter, in the next eighteen years, published eight novels, a novelette, several stories, and an article or so. His *The Light in the Forest* (1953), a story of Indian captivity, sold to Walt Disney Studios for filming for motion pictures and television; its sequel *A Country of Strangers* was published in 1966. Still other Richter novels of the period: *The Mountain on the Desert* (1955), a heavily philosophical work; *The Lady* (1957), the author's final southwestern novel; *The Waters of Kronos* (1960) and *A Simple Honorable Man* (1962), first two volumes of an uncompleted autobiographical trilogy; *The Grandfathers* (1964); and *The Aristocrat* (1968). The folkloric novelette, *Over the Blue Mountain* (1967), appeals especially to young readers even though it is a cut above most works written for children. Of those publications between 1950 and 1968, the most notable are *The Waters of Kronos*, recipient of the 1960 National Book Award for fiction, and its sequel *A Simple Honorable Man*.

After more than half a century of productive writing, Conrad Richter died 30 October 1968. Four years later, his widow Harvena Achenbach Richter died 7 March 1972. Both are buried in Pine Grove.

Homes and the Writer

As well as his family backgrounds, the places of Richter's residence shaped his writing. Those included the Pine Grove of his birth and the Albuquerque of his first truly successful fictional works.

Anachronistic to the *Harrisburg* Turnpike from which it departs, a road meanders northward through rye, barley, and wheat meadows rolling gently to the pine- and hemlock-dotted slopes of Blue Mountain. Across the summit and from the base of the blue-green walls separating it from the outside, a pine grove lies hushed in much the same fashion it must have done when the first German settler arrived more than two centuries ago. The tranquillity of the contemporary scene belies the antiquity of civilization in Pine Grove, Pennsylvania, and complements the great ash trees, lindens, and horse chestnuts that frame pleasant houses along the streets. In such a house once resided Conrad Richter, whose fiction and essays in part quietly celebrate elemental nature and decry human efforts that despoil it.

Of the Pine Grove in which he was born, Richter wrote, "I think sometimes that if our small town might have been fenced off and preserved exactly as it was, with its characters still alive and doing their stuff, it would be known today from coast to coast."[21] In a similar vein, he further expressed intense feeling for his native state: "To the very young boy [Richter himself], the word Pennsylvania meant the world. He saw the red-brick house that he and his brothers were born in, and the house was Pennsylvania. He looked at the blue-green mountain walls rimming his home town. . . . He waded in the Old Lutheran Church run."[22]

Pine Grove in the 1890s was a farming community in Schuylkill County on the southern edge of the anthracite coal region. Such of Conrad Richter's novels as *Always Young and Fair, The Waters of Kronos, A Simple Honorable Man,* and *The Aristocrat,* as well as numerous short stories, are set here (the name is changed to Pine Mills and Unionville) and deal extensively with farming and mining. Moreover, the natural beauty of the village provides material for Richter's nonfiction, as well as for his novels and stories. "Each spring," Richter recalled in an article, "my father used to mail a shoebox full of arbutus to an old friend who had moved away but pined to see and smell" Pennsylvania again.[23] The mountains, Pennsylvania's "ancient symbol of freedom," as Richter saw them, moved the author as a youngster "most deeply."

Nearly three-quarters of a century after his childhood, Richter, in the autobiographical novel *The Waters of Kronos,* suggests the haunting effect the mountains had upon him: "The road turned and Shade [or Blue] Mountain stood framed in the windshield. As a boy he [John Donner or Richter himself] had felt mixed emotions for that long forested wall shutting him and Unionville [Pine Grove] from the world. He had thought it high, wild and almost impassable then. Later, after the lofty ranges of the West, it had seemed little more than a hill. But, curiously, it stood high and wild again today."[24]

The "spirit of place" as an influence on Richter's works includes also the tenor of the times. During the decade of Richter's birth (1890s), as Frederick Jackson Turner demonstrated, the American frontier passed from existence. Farm strife from falling prices and rising interest rates led to the formation of the Populist party. Industrial strife was represented by the Carnegie steel strike at Homestead, Pennsylvania, and by the Pullman Palace Car Company strike in Illinois. The stock market collapsed; rural banks failed; Coxey's "army" marched on Washington. But by 1896 the crisis passed, and soon the Spanish-American War ushered in an era of American imperialism. On the lighter side could be counted the horseless carriage and the Gibson girls.

Much of the spirit of these times Richter weaves into his novel *Always Young and Fair,* which begins about the time of the Spanish-American War and ends shortly after World War I. In that novel and in the short story "Good Neighbors," Pine Grove is Pine Mills; but in *The Waters of Kronos, A Simple Honorable Man,* and *The Aristocrat* it is Unionville. The houses of Miss Augusta R. Filbert, a cousin by marriage to Richter, and of her uncle Dan provide the background for *Always Young and Fair* and for *A Simple Honorable Man,* in the latter of which Miss Filbert is the character Georgia. Finally, Pine Grove and environs figure indirectly in several of Richter's earliest short stories that usually are set both in a city and in a small town. The "Penn City" and "Pennver" of the early stories suggest Philadelphia and Pittsburgh.

The Pennsylvania Dutch country around Pine Grove provides the setting for Richter's story "The Last Man Alive," which concerns the Amish. And Richter's brother Frederick's home, Syracuse, New York, is the setting for part of the story "Tempered Copper," while his brother Joseph's home, Reading (spelled "Redding"), is the setting of the story "Swanson's 'Home Sweet Home' " and of part of the novel *A Simple Honorable Man.*

Selinsgrove, where Richter's father attended Susquehanna College, becomes Port Oxford; and Susquehanna, West Shore College, in *A Simple Honorable Man*. During the course of his ministry, Richter's father served seven parishes. Tremont and Donaldson, his first charge, correspond, in *A Simple Honorable Man,* to Mahanoy and Lost Run. From Tremont and Donaldson, the minister moved to six other parishes, one of them twice. And one of his moves took his family to a hard-coal town at the foot of what was known as "Fighting Hill," where, during a strike, women tore one another's hair. "Fighting Hill" is a model for a portion of Richter's novel *Tacey Cromwell* and for the setting of his short story "The Marriage That Couldn't Succeed."

From 1907 to 1910, Richter's father was at White Deer Valley in Lycoming County, ten miles from Williamsport, serving churches corresponding, in *A Simple Honorable Man,* to Manada Hill, Frame Church, and Spring Garden Church and, in *The Waters of Kronos,* to White Rose Valley parish. In 1910, Richter's father moved to Scalp Level parish in Cambria County, represented in fiction by Paint Creek and Chadd's Cove—site of Harry Donner's (John Richter's) ministry until retirement. In succeeding years, he served, from 1912 to 1916, at St. Peter's in Reading; for a few months in the Cairnbrook parish in Somerset County; at Christ Church, Milton, which, with 448 communicants in 1917, constituted his largest congregation; and, until 1926, at St. Matthew's in Allentown. These latter charges figure only incidentally in Conrad Richter's fiction.

One place nearby and two places remote to Pennsylvania figure in novels and stories growing out of Richter's youthful itineracy. Western Maryland is the setting of *The Grandfathers*. The Coeur d'Alene region of Idaho provides setting and other details for "The Girl That 'Got' Colly," a mining story, and Spokane, as well as Coeur d'Alene, furnishes the background for Richter's first short story, "How Tuck Went Home."

From 1922 to 1928, Richter and his family (including their New-foundland dog "Brimsey") resided in a 150-year-old farm house on the land of the first settler in Clarks Valley near Harrisburg. In a magazine article, Richter described the area as a "haunting landscape" that afforded beauty and peace. Especially appealing were "scene after scene out of olden days, unfenced woods, parklike banks and tree meadows unspoiled by man." Those qualities and others produced what the author called an "indefinable something."[25]

This "indefinable something" Richter ultimately decided to be possibly "intimations" that the "Clarks Valley folks in their pocket of land shut

off by mountains from the rest of the world, where in our lifetime the
essences which our fathers had lived by and which had been the
'dwelling place' of the race for countless generations still flourished along
with the old uncontaminated ways and poetic expression of commonplace
things."[26] But whether the virtues were actual or merely "intimations,"
they were repeatedly expressed in Richter's fiction. Among the examples
are such stories as "Cabbages and Shoes," "Forest Mould," "Suicide,"
"Rich Relations," "Over the Hill to the Rich House," "The Man Who
Loved a Hound," and "The Man Who Retired."

Among the people of Clarks Valley, Jim Dell was the son of a
father who had been coachman at the Peter Allen house. There in the
late 1600s Indian girls had danced and bounties for Indian scalps had
been paid. Richter undoubtedly had these early events in mind in
writing the novels *The Light in the Forest and A Country of Strangers.*

The critical illness that almost claimed the life of his wife compelled
Richter and his family to move in 1928 from Pennsylvania to New
Mexico. In Albuquerque and environs, Richter found a place diametrically
opposite to anything he had known. But, as Richter said, the Southwest
is a country not easily loved, and so loved the more deeply. Thus, in
The Mountain on the Desert, the author wrote: "I've often asked myself,
why do we feel about our Southwestern country as we do? On first
being exiled here we may fiercely dislike it. Let us stay awhile and we
can scarcely bear to leave it. Away from it, we seldom fail to remember
it without longing."[27]

Richter's attachment to Albuquerque, Santa Fe, and Taos was due
partly to what he was to call their "greatest charm"—their quality that
"lets the visitor drop the fatigue of the familiar and 'begin all over
again with nothing to carry over from the past,' as Gide wrote when
he first went to Africa."[28] Or, as Richter said in a letter to the late
Walter S. Campbell: "In my own case, the most helpful thing I found
in writing of the Southwest was the Southwest itself, its brilliant light,
wide spaces, mountains and deserts, particularly its great sky and finer
air which lift a man into a more rarefied and stimulating world of life
and thought inhabited by certain lesser gods called Southwesterners."[29]

Certainly, the Southwest was to enable him to turn his hand to the
best fiction of which he was capable, for it provided him with the
materials for his first novel, *The Sea of Grass,* as well as the earlier
collection of short stories, *Early Americana;* the later historical novels,
Tacey Cromwell and The Lady; and the philosophical novel *The Mountain
on the Desert.*

Chapter Two
Energy and Harmony

"The great question as to a poet or a novelist," Henry James said, "is, How does he feel about life? What, in the last analysis, is his philosophy?" For the usual writer, the answer to James's question perforce comes "in the last analysis." Whether evolving gradually in a straight line or proceeding in a manner resembling the peaks and valleys of a business graph, one's philosophy ordinarily is a lifetime process of becoming. Not until the final judgments have been expressed by an author can it be said with relative certainty what his or her view of life is.

With Conrad Richter, however, something of the reverse is true. As if to settle the matter at the onset of his career, he set forth his basic theories of life in the book-length essay *Human Vibration* (1925). Then, following his technique of "observation, interpretation, and check," he refined his philosophy in two subsequent companion pieces—the long essay *Principles in Bio-Physics* (1927) and the philosophical novel *The Mountain on the Desert* (1955).[1] Richter's more than fifty fictional stories, novels, and other writing following *Human Vibration* amounted in part to a continual reaffirmation of his philosophy.

In developing his theories about the workings of human life and mind, Richter was responding to intellectual currents of the times: the clash between orthodox Christian religion, which he had painfully rejected, and science—most notably Darwinian evolutionary theory and its implications for human life, advances in physical sciences, and Freudian and related clinical psychology. He viewed his ideas as something of an attempt, figuratively speaking, to reconcile physics and metaphysics.

Philosophical Theories

Human Vibration represents his first attempt to articulate principles that evolved from investigations dating, Richter said, to about 1913. Proceeding in the manner of the analytical chemist and physicist, the author claims to be undertaking an explanation of "the individuality

17

of human character and reaction"—"the mechanics of life and mind."
All "life and matter," he says, "is but the effect of mechanical, that
is to say, natural laws." (The term *mechanics*, as Richter pointed out
years later, was something of an unfortunate choice and not to be
confused with mechanistic naturalism: "If ever I use the term 'mechanism,' it doesn't follow that it's purely mechanical. By mechanism I
mean that it uses energy, its physical parts, its so-called mental parts,
and any possible finer instrument connected with it whose substance
and purpose are unknown."[2] Under such mechanical or "natural laws,"
the individual is something of a human storage battery whose physical
and mental actions are determined by three primary elements: (1) *cells*
with vibratory fluctuations regulated by the availability of (2) *cellular
energy* which, in turn, is influenced by (3) *forces opposing the free
replenishment* of the energy.

By "cell" Richter means not necessarily the "biological term, but
the minute life unit through countless numbers of which in each
individual the living organism spends its energy."[3] But, if the cell
admits of being understood, its energy does not. That is to say, rather,
that the source of energy—*nerve energy, psychic energy, life energy, pep,*
or *strength* are different names for the same force—remains an enigma
except that "the body refines it from certain raw products."[4] Indeed,
if "one of us should invent a method of pouring it into the human
system without shock," says Richter, "such mortal enemies as age, pain,
depression, weakness and premature death could be postponed almost
to the point of elimination."[5]

As it is, however, the free replenishment of cellular energy is thwarted
by high expenditure and by insufficient production. Such opposition,
says Richter, "is the plan of life, blind or intelligent," and is so ordered
"that the energy refined by an organism is generally inadequate to its
demands."[6] As a result, physical and psychological inharmonies plague
people. "Inharmonious thoughts are persistently more conscious than
harmonious thoughts," contends Richter. "The world must try to be
happy—to forget unhappiness. Disappointment, discouragement, grief,
and a thousand and one other forms of high vibration rate often
tyrannize consciousness for days, sometimes longer."[7]

Inharmony, or lean energy flow, however, often has compensatory
effects in that it can contribute paradoxically to the evolutionary process
through which humans continue to change for the better physically and
psychologically. Harmony, or full energy flow, is conducive to static

satisfaction, but inharmony can result in the organism's summoning energy reserves in amounts sufficient to lead it to new vibratory heights. The process of evolution, according to Richter, "is not the physical development of a tail or a fin, but mental development of the collective vibration rates of an organism."[8] Its lower stages are represented by physical battle for life and "for possession and escape from enemy. Higher in evolution the battles are often mental."[9] Thus, sympathy for "others, understanding of their inharmony, even appreciation of their lack of higher harmony which they do not realize themselves, is the mark of evolutionary progress."[10]

Their mechanistic qualities notwithstanding, Richter's theories of life, he says, do "not imply that there is no Supreme Intelligence" or God: they simply mean that "there is no mystery, only mechanical laws which we have not as yet grasped."[11] In his two book-length essays and the philosophical novel, Richter does not elaborate on that matter. In an interview, however, he said that the "powers that be" are "infinitely far ahead of us, that we can only know certain small hints of them, that we have infinitely far to go," and that all humanity probably travels "the same road." With Lafcadio Hearn, Richter agreed that "cognition" actually is "recognition." The higher powers, Richter concluded, are "worth following" because of their promotion of such spiritual qualities as "love, care, wanting to share."[12]

Principles in Bio-Physics, published in paperback in 1927 two years after *Human Vibration,* reiterates many of the basic concepts but adds new dimensions. One of the added features consists of a set of symbols for the three life elements articulated in the earlier work. The letter A represents the cell's energy voltage; B, resistance in cell and circuit; A/B, energy flow or current; and C, expenditure rate or vibration pitch. The cell's voltage, "its bio-electrical motive force," explains Richter, is "the pressure of its life energy."[13] Resistance is that of "non-conducting material in the cell and circuits, which includes the resistance placed by nature on the removal of that resistance."[14] Energy flow is "a current of energy originating in the lipoid membranes of the cell and passing over a mortal circuit. It is symbolized A/B because its strength is literally A divided by B, the voltage of the cell divided by the resistance in the cell and its circuit."[15] And expenditure rate is "the expending rate of a cell, its frequency of vibration."[16] Still another new dimension to Richter's philosophy, as set forth in *Principles in Bio-Physics* is the presentation in detail of the functions of the "circuit," the device connecting the cells of the organism with one another. "Through inheritance from literally countless ancestors across an incredible period of time, and to a minor extent from individual experience," explains Richter, "the trillions of cells in each individual have been joined by a stupendous network of nerve matter of various degree and also by other connecting and conducting substances native to the life organism."[17] In thus detailing the "circuit" and describing the processes through which energy flows over it, Richter prepares the way for an even more thorough analysis of these functions in *The Mountain on the Desert.* And in insisting that all "mortal organisms" experience the "automatic urge to get from inharmony to harmony,"[18] *Principles in Bio-Physics* reiterates a key point in *Human Vibration:* the harmony of today is the direct product of the inharmony of yesterday.

During the twenty-eight years between *Principles in Bio-Physics* and *The Mountain on the Desert* (1955), his philosophical novel, Richter continually applied his technique of "observation, interpretation, and check." In addition to its advantage of perspective, its structure places *The Mountain on the Desert* decidedly above the earlier companion works. Gone is the quasi-scientific approach that is wholly expository. As if acknowledging the failure of the earlier essays, Richter, through a character, says, "Electric analogies are closer to the psycho-energic processes but they involve terms and conceptions the rest of our friends here won't understand."[19]

Instead, *The Mountain on the Desert* spins a narrative thread—albeit a weak one—that binds Socratic dialogues among a hermit and a group of inquiring college students. The narrative is set in San Antonito, near Albuquerque. Here resides the hermit, a seer named Michael, who has forsaken the success of the material world that surely would have accrued to one of his superior intelligence and who has instead assumed the simple existence of a rug weaver.[20] Christ-like Michael administers to the physical and psychical needs of Mexican peasants, thus creating a reputation that attracts the college students to him. Among the cosmopolitan group of young seekers are one given to moods of depression, a stammerer, a Mohammedan, and a blind poet. And to them Michael reveals through precept and example his theories which Richter now calls "psycho-energics' but are actually the same concepts of the supply and expenditure of energy seen in earlier works. *The Mountain on the Desert* goes beyond its predecessors, however, by describing energy-release processes in children, adults, language, music, beauty, and neuroses. Moreover, it introduces a new dimension by speculating on energy supply and expenditure as they might apply to a life after death.

Reiterating that the individual's mind and body are both "the energy-providing plant and spending instrument," the novel singles out limited energy as the distinguishing feature of life. Thus, energy hunger becomes the "basic primal motive" for humans, who "consciously or unconsciously" hunger "for energy night and day."[21] Since people live "in an energy-limited world with many kinds of personal deficiencies," they must seek to supply these deficiencies by releasing energy from themselves.[22] Many of the energy-release processes "are instinctive, handed down in the egg. Some are learned."[23] The inherited ones ordinarily are geared to the five senses, of which sight is the superior.

Physical exercise is one of the best therapeutic release processes, as well as one "of the most ancient and common;" because, contrary to popular opinion, energy does not beget activity but rather results from it.[24] For this reason, creative growth may result from external causes such as hardships, but it may also stem from self-discipline—the self-administering of hardship. "One reason man has gone so much farther with material and mechanistic things than he has with himself," Richter says, "is that he isn't bound by the temporal welfare or pleasure of the material or machine."[25] Whereas individuals put matter through extreme heat, pressure, and other tests, they cannot and do not subject themselves to such trials.

Crying, swearing, laughing, and praying are still other release processes. Whatever the device, the result is an energy transfer: one cell group alarms another, thus setting off energy which it robs. The life impulse is "the basic hunger of primary cell groups for more energy and their consequent incitement of secondary groups to spend energy so the primary groups can get hold of some of it."[26] Even relaxation requires an expenditure of energy which one must obtain, if not from the normal reservoir then from some other, before one can relax.

In summary, *Human Vibration, Principles in Bio-Physics,* and *The Mountain on the Desert* hold that humans function mentally (both consciously and subconsciously) and physically in response to cellular vibrations fed by psychical and physical energy. If energy is plentiful, the human mechanism performs harmoniously. The highest manifestations of such harmony are love and understanding. On the other hand, if energy levels are low, the human machine is out of sorts. Conflict with other people and nature is a sure sign of such deficiency. To satisfy their energy hunger, humans must engage in intense activity, which causes the stronger cells in the body, as it were, to overflow and reenergize the weaker cells. The process somewhat resembles the working of an automotive storage battery that has been built up by the running of the vehicle's jump-started engine.

In formulating his views of life, Richter draws only obliquely on discernible philosophical tradition for intellectual authority. Isolated fragments of his thought occasionally invite comparison with classical mechanism, deism, Bergsonian vitalism, Jungian psychology, Couéism, New Thought, and Christian Science. But, in virtually every instance, the temptation to draw a comparison is quickly discouraged by a preponderance of dissimilarity.

A somewhat more evident affiliation becomes apparent in *Human Vibration,* which Richter prefaces with a quotation from Michael Faraday: "The world little knows how many of the thoughts and theories which have passed through the mind of a scientific investigator have been crushed in silence and secrecy by his own severe criticism and adverse examination; that in the most successful instances not a tenth of the suggestions, the hopes, the wishes, the preliminary conclusions have been reached."

Faraday's first of two basic laws suggests that the amount of chemical action produced by an electric current in electrolysis is directly proportionate to the quantity of electricity that passes through the circuit. And the concept, although applied to a field different from human life, has strong affinity with Richter's theory of cellular energy in conflict with opposing factors. Yet the prefatory quotation more nearly implies what Richter confirms in stating that he, like Faraday, feels his conclusions to be tentative or at least incompletely articulated. "I have no pretense that everything I have 'found' is final," Richter said in 1925. "I believe we have got to a new bottom, but it should be folly to claim that there will be no additions and corrections from other minds."[27]

Again, a link between Richter and a philosophical tradition—that of G. W. Crile—becomes evident in *Principles in Bio-Physics,* which alludes frequently to Crile's bipolar theory of living organisms. In approximating Crile, however, Richter makes clear a basic distinction between the two. Contrary to Crile, he says, "I have found no evidence for a mechanistic doctrine that life phenomena are caused alone by the simple overflow of energy, governed by the increased or decreased conductivity from gland discharge."[28]

Actually, Richter's philosophy of life is a heterogeneous mixture of concepts. If one were determined to link Richter to a traditional philosophical movement, therefore, one might seize on this diversity of ideas (not infrequently conflicting) and on Richter's penchant for alluding to Emerson, Thoreau, and John Burroughs as signs of a loose affiliation with idealism.

In effect, what Richter is doing on one level in these theories is reaffirming established scientific theory: that the human being, like all animals, is an organism with mechanical qualities. Yet, recognizing further that, while science has explored with considerable success certain aspects of the condition, it has left unanswered the larger questions—recognizing this fundamental limitation, that is, Richter seeks to explain how mind inhabits the body and to show the relationship between the material and the higher levels of human existence.

His theories serve Richter well in enabling him to perceive the limitations of science. They fail him, however, to the extent—indeed extensive—that they defy demonstration either by scientific or metaphysical procedure. For this reason, one can agree with Joseph Wood Krutch's estimate of Richter's philosophy: "There are truths which poetry has approached more closely than science and which are better adumbrated by analogies than stated propositions. But I doubt that the poet is wise when he borrows a specific terminology from science and then uses it in a sense which science does not recognize or when he attempts to identify analogy with proposition."[29]

But, if the philosophical essays and novel fail intellectually, they still perform at least two useful services. One is that they demonstrate, as Frederic I. Carpenter reminds us, that Richter's mind "has always sought to analyze and to explain human phenomena through conscious symbols and that he has always rejected the simple philosophy of mechanistic naturalism."[30] The other and more fundamental service is that the essays inform Richter's fiction, providing a key to his thematic unity and to the more distinctive aspects of his art.

The relationship between his philosophy and his fiction Richter emphasizes in the foreword to *The Mountain on the Desert*. His philosophical works, he says, were not written "to explain or further develop" his novels. Rather, the reverse is true: the fictional works were designed in part to illustrate his philosophy. Be that as it may, it is important to note that, in building his fiction on those tenuous philosophical concepts, Richter writes better than he knows. That is to say that his artistry overshadows the limitation of his thought, creating an impressive body of works that transcend their foundations.

The correlation between Richter's philosophical works and his fiction, however, has not been generally recognized. Indeed, the prevailing tendency has been to view the two genres as totally unrelated—a tendency implicit in the evaluation one reviewer makes of *The Mountain on the Desert* by contending that "these dialogues will interest students of occult religions more than readers of Richter's novels."[31] Such a tendency is evident even in the thinking of one of the early scholars of Richter's works. Bruce Sutherland, after summarizing *Human Vibration* and *Principles in Bio-Physics,* concludes that the essays merely help explain Richter's interest in pioneer virtues.[32]

Contributing to this widespread temptation to disassociate Richter's essays from his fiction are two factors. One, the theories articulated in the essays ordinarily appear only inferentially in the stories and novels. As Richter himself says, they are *overtones.* The other factor obscuring the author's intent is his own artistic mastery. The simplicity of style, concision of presentation, and vividness of portrayal of character, event, and setting—qualities for which Richter has been praised most often—tend to draw attention to themselves and away from even the fictional themes. And, when this tendency is coupled with the prosaic quality of the themes, particularly in the early stories and in the later minor novels, the obscuration of intent becomes even more pronounced. Yet the cumulative meanings growing out of the fictional materials actually have their roots in Richter's philosophical works. These fictional themes, in other words, are the *undertones* relating to the *overtones.*

The essays in the main have physiological and psychological implications, but they also have mystical ones. For this reason, the fiction representing them likewise assumes multiple levels of meaning. Richter may consciously or otherwise intend for his themes to take ritualistic, mythical, and mystical directions to be consistent with his philosophical theories. Or the deeper levels of meaning may merely develop naturally. In either event, the process works like this: illustrative of the theory that all life and matter are governed by mechanical, or natural, laws—a concept articulated in the essays and philosophical novel—is the fictional theme of the organic unity of humans and nature. On the physical level, Richter develops this theme by revealing humans in close harmony with the land and, occasionally, with animals. Realistically, however, he sometimes shows the reverse side of the coin—the hostility of nature to humans. But this opposite emphasis, illustrated principally by drought that destroys farm crops and livestock (the corollary theme of the life and death of the land), does not dispute the veracity of the organic relationship so much as it verifies the ambivalence of it. Nature and the human being, like brother and brother, Richter is saying, may be organically related and still not always get along well together. On the psychological and mystical levels, the theme of organic unity promotes such corollaries as the idyll of the farm (an agrarian myth celebrating the superiority of rural life to urban) and the mystique of the wilderness (a theme closely related to, but more mystical than, the idyll of the farm).

Representative of Richter's philosophical theories of human energy expenditure and supply are fictional themes emerging from the processes of "westering." In stories and novels set in the Southwest, Richter first takes up the march of civilization from wilderness to farm (or ranch) to town. But in works set in Pennsylvania and Ohio he actually first completes the cycle. On the physio-psychological level, the wilderness stage of "westering" produces such themes as restless wandering and the hunter's drive in conflict with the settler's instinct. Both are suggestive of the theory of "inharmony" or energy hunger, as advanced in the essays. The farming (or ranching) and the community stages of "westering," paralleling Richter's philosophical concepts of evolutionary progress, advance the themes of human prevalence and of historical change. Ancillary to the first are the themes of altruism, world understanding and brotherhood, and hardship-into-gain.

All three, however, do not emerge exclusively from the processes of "westering." They appear also as dominant themes in Richter's nonhistorical fiction. Then, inasmuch as all people do not endure and prevail, Richter realistically adds still other corollary themes: the tragedy of youthful death, loneliness, the inability of eastern woman to adjust to frontier life, the eager heart rejected, and the detriment of overly protective parents to the individual. Again, the last two do not pertain exclusively to fiction dealing with "westering," but appear as well in nonhistorical works. Themes subordinate, but related, to historical change are America as an ethnic melting pot, the old way in conflict with the new, the mixed allegiance of an individual to two ethnic groups, freedom versus restraint, and the duality of civilization that is at once good and evil.

Finally, the psychological-mystical level of the three stages of "westering" builds up the myths of the rite de passage and of the making of the American racial unconscious from the dark night of the soul to gradual illumination. It also promotes the more mystical themes of the search for the Spiritual Father, the search for individual identity, time, and the assumption of guilt. All four of these, however, appear also in Richter's fiction unrelated to the processes of "westering."

Organic Style

At least three circumstances, in Malcolm Cowley's opinion, must be present in the life of a person before he or she is apt to become a creative writer. They are intensive reading, a feeling of loneliness, and a desire for public approval.[33] In his own case, Conrad Richter said, intensive reading most certainly influenced him. To a somewhat lesser extent, loneliness "and perhaps the 'non-simpaticoness' of others" played parts. A desire for public approval, however, did not motivate him nearly so much as the desire for self-approval.[34]

As to other writers most influential on him, Richter cited Emerson, Thoreau, and John Burroughs, whom, he said, he tried unsuccessfully to emulate; John Fox, Jr., Robert Chambers, Willa Cather, and W. H. Hudson. Cather's treatment of character and background impressed Richter particularly as being fundamentally sound. But Hudson impressed Richter most of all.[35]

The intensive reading Richter did as boy and man provides a key to his theories of art. In a manuscript prepared for radio broadcast on W. H. Hudson's *Far Away and Long Ago,* Richter focuses on those artistic qualities in Hudson that square with his own concepts. Among them are the necessity to transfer feeling, to rewrite carefully, to utilize an organic style (frequently including symbolism), to be selective, to arrange materials carefully, and to employ a conditioned point of view. And to these he had added (earlier in *The Mountain on the Desert,* as well as later in an interview) what to him is the essential element of energy, a concept recalling ideas expressed in his philosophical writing.

In appraising the work of Hudson, Richter cites deft transferal as the "ability to make an experience and loving observation" of the writer also an "experience and loving observation of the reader." He thus implies what, in an interview and in a preface, he expressed as the "chief thing" for himself: "recognition. Some might call it a critical sense. There must be a striving to set down [to transfer] the words so the reader or myself gets the impression in my mind."[36]

Sometimes, as Richter admits may have been the case with Hudson, the "recognition" may simply be "the longing of an old man for his youth in a country many thousands of miles away and in a time now completely vanished and which therefore could never be revisited or relived." Or, again, "recognition" might even be "a dispensation of the gods."[37] But, whatever its nature, "recognition"—this "impression," this "feeling the writer had for a place and person"—in Richter's judgment is difficult to transfer: "As a rule, life and nature are so much more real and vivid than the reflection that finds its way on paper. Many times, in my case at least, the attempted transfer fails."[38]

Whether the transfer succeeds or fails depends often on the rewriting, which in his own case Richter felt he sometimes overdid. Illustrating his tendency with a metaphor drawn from broom-handle making, Richter said he could fancy his subconscious self taunting his conscious being with the accusation that he "polished that handle so carefully." In actuality, however, he explained, it is not "polishing at all, but getting it where it falls into the critical image" in his mind.[39]

Again, the success of the transfer depends upon an organic or indigenous writing style, the salient features of which Richter explains in *The Mountain on the Desert*. "Language releases energy" in the speaker. The more "effective the language," therefore, "the more effective the energy release."[40] ("There must be this flow of energy," Richter said in an interview, "pushing for it [the work] so it not only comes in the first place but persists.")[41] In other words, the chief purpose of language is not so much to communicate as "to release energy to the speaker."[42] But "the words a man uses and the way he places them together control energy responses" also in the listener.[43] ("A good novel or story," Richter said in an interview, "should happen to do one thing, manage the reader's energy flow.")[44] The success of communication, then, depends upon the effectiveness of the writer in creating energy release in the reader through vivid descriptions, compression of style, arrangement of materials, and the evocation of word pictures (images) appealing to the senses.

In certain respects, Richter's theory of organic style, influenced as it is by the concept of energy flow, coincides with ideas of Emerson and, earlier, Coleridge. The latter, in discussing the organic principle of writing upon which Emerson also built, insisted that a work shapes itself as it develops from "within, and the fulness of its development is one and the same with the perfection of its outward form."[45]

Evident in Richter's concepts of style is the necessity of symbolism. Such a requisite becomes pronounced in Richter's estimate of Hudson's work to which symbolism gives "unsuspected depth": "The death of an old dog stirs up in the reader wonder of the meaning of life. The confession of a gaucho leaves profound reflections on the question of immortality. Hudson's mystical feeling as a boy for the tree as a living and breathing being like himself is a blinding insight into the unknown forces that bind all life together."[46]

Finally, the transfer of feeling succeeds partly, Richter said in an interview, through the author's use of careful selectivity and arrangement: "The novelist can use only a fraction of what real life he knows. The rest must be imagined in the development of his story." As to arrangement, "In life things, incidents, thoughts happen any time. It isn't till the middle of the night as a rule that they fall into their proper place and perspective. In life it [arrangement] is not necessary. You can't throw down your life so easy and pick up another. You must live through things or their memory. But in writing they must sustain the reader's interest and give flesh and emotion to the right junctures."[47]

In appraising Hudson's work, Richter dwells on point of view, suggesting that one reads *Far Away and Long Ago* with the conviction that the book could never have been written at the time these incidents occurred but only when seen back through the soft glow of a long and exceptional life."[48] Such a middle-distance perspective Richter himself utilized extensively, particularly in his historical stories and novels. It is well suited to novels of violence in that the limited point of view mutes the sordid aspects that were repugnant to Richter's sensitivity. Moreover, the middle-distance point of view allowed Richter often to utilize narrators who were related to the protagonists but removed enough in time to be objective.

The various facets of Richter's theory of organic style in writing prove consonant with his philosophical theories of life generally. In the application of both sets of theories in his essays, novels, and stories, as previously suggested, however, Richter proved more successful as a stylist than as a philosophical thinker. That is to say again that his organic style of writing transcends the limitations of the philosophy that Richter espoused, a philosophy that he considered to be the "overtones" of all that he wrote.

Chapter Three
Altruism and Expiation

Conrad Richter grew to manhood and published his first fiction during the fin de siècle. Another name for the era, "the genteel age," signified a period of prosperity, the fervent nationalism of Teddy Roosevelt, and (despite inroads made by early naturalists) Victorian literature. Soon, however, World War I and the Roaring Twenties that followed it displaced the "gentility" of national life and the Victorian qualities of national letters. Replacing gentility were the liberality and cynicism of newly emancipated youth, who, in an age of quick wealth, indulged themselves freely in bathtub gin, jazz, and the Charleston. In literature, the new way of life gave rise to either applause for or criticism of the times. But whether advocates or critics, writers evidenced strong tendencies toward experimentation in technique and innovation in content.

Having launched his career in the tranquil waters of Victorianism, Richter mostly ignored the literary drift of the war and postwar periods, and he maintained his original course for about two decades. Such authorial navigation thus avoided innovation in technique and content, but it did admit occasionally of criticism. Especially did the physical and mental softness of youth disturb him and draw his verbal fire. For the most part, however, the twenty-five or more stories Richter published between 1913 and 1933, when actually he was serving his apprenticeship as a writer, represent concessions to popular taste. The earmarks of the novice and the popularizer are readily observable in melodramatic plots with whimsical or trick endings, type characters, and conventional themes.

Providing outlets for these early stories were more than a dozen magazines, one collection of Richter's own, and collections of at least three others. The magazines varied from pulps to such commercial giants as *Ladies' Home Journal,* the *Saturday Evening Post,* and *American.* From them Richter drew twelve of his pieces into his first collected volume, *Brothers of No Kin and Other Stories* (1924). In the process, he altered three of the titles, changing "The Making of 'Val' Pierce" (*American,* April 1920) to "Forest Mould"; "The Man Who Hid Himself" (*American,* July 1920) to "Suicide"; and "You're Too Con-

twisted Satisfied—Jim Ted!" (*American,* February 1921) to "Bad Luck
is Good Luck."

Brothers of No Kin epitomizes Richter's stories of the first two decades,
but a somewhat necessary orientation to an investigation of this collected
volume is an examination of the author's first published story. "How
Tuck Went Home" appeared 6 September 1913 in *Cavalier,* and it
established patterns from which most of its early successors would be
cut. Its plot, for example, is typically melodramatic. Blinded and dying
from injuries in a mine explosion, a young man named Tuck expresses
a final wish to experience the sounds and smells of a city such as his
native New York. Moved by the request, his two rough companions,
Mike and Jud, promise to take Tuck to Spokane. But as they make
the promise, they realize that the trek would be too difficult for Tuck.
Placing the dying man on a mule tied to a tree, then, the companions
pretend the trip by walking the animal in a circle. To make the altruistic
hoax realistic, they simulate sounds and smells of the city. On the fifth
day, when the cortege supposedly has reached its destination, Tuck asks
to be taken to a church to die. The narrator, a descendant of ministers,
agrees to assume the role of a clergyman. To him Tuck confesses
privately that he knows the undertaking has been a hoax but pledges
the narrator to secrecy to salve the feelings of Mike and Jud. He
requests that he be buried beneath the tree to which the mule has
been tied.

Here, for plot, characters, and setting, Richter has relied upon the
mining experience and the miners he had known during his investigation
in the Coeur d'Alene region of Idaho. Because of authorial immaturity,
however, he is unable to employ these materials in a fresh manner and
thus avoid typed characters. In relating his narrator to ministerial
antecedents, he alludes for the first time in fiction to his own family's
clergymen. Such reliance upon personal materials continued with steadily
increasing frequency and constantly improving technique to characterize
his works.

The hoax of the characters Mike and Jud, in "How Tuck Went
Home," promotes the conventional theme of altruism, a concept that
appears repeatedly in Richter's fiction. What makes the theme noteworthy, however, is not its familiarity nor its frequency of usage, but
its relationship to one of the author's key theories of life. In the
philosophical works, the high mark of evolutionary progress is the
acquiring of understanding and love for which altruism is but another
name.

Thematically, the corpus of Richter's fiction suggests the gradual development of the concepts of evolution from the lowest to the highest levels. Thus, the early representation of the high mark (altruism) in "How Tuck Went Home" amounts to the author's starting in thematic reverse. Richter probably began with the last stage of the process out of which the theme of altruism grows because it was the nearest to his own time and hence the most readily observable. Too, at the time he employed it, he was still struggling to articulate the theories in the essays.

The title story for the collection *Brothers of No Kin* had been the first to bring Richter extensive recognition. Like the earlier "How Tuck Went Home," "Brothers of No Kin" revolves around an act of altruism; but it affords a mystical dimension. In "How Tuck Went Home," the altruism takes the form of relatively simple good deeds, but in "Brothers of No Kin" it emerges as one man's assuming the sins of another. Anterior to the story, Jeremiah Ritter and Ebenezer Straint, despite their differences of personality, are friends—"brothers of no kin." At the age of twenty-three, Jerry Ritter left Heisler Cove, Pennsylvania, and for thirty-five years wandered the face of the earth. At least once a year, nevertheless, he sent letters and small packages back to his old friend Ebenezer. As the story proper opens, it has been several years since Ebenezer has heard from Jerry. The night before his disappearance more than thirty-five years before, Jerry had left behind "an empty whiskey jug gotten God knows where, and two battered sons of the Cove's church trustees" (that is, he got drunk and beat them). One of the victims, Billy Houser, had died from the injuries. Each year Ebenezer has gone to the cemetery before Ascension Day and tended the grave of the murdered youth. He has done this in response to a request Jerry had made in an early letter. Finally, one night in February a gaunt and dying Jerry returns to Heisler Cove. Recognizing the indigent by his familiar greeting of "Red," Ebenezer takes Jerry into his own home. In April, Ebenezer finds Jerry cowering against the wall of his sick room, fearing that he will die before the day is over. Jerry confesses to Ebenezer that he has killed others in addition to Billy Houser and that he has otherwise led a life of crime. Ebenezer insists that Jerry accompany him to church, where Ebenezer prays that Jerry may reap his (Ebenezer's) rewards in heaven and that he (Ebenezer) may assume Jerry's sins. Then Ebenezer sells his land and all other possessions, sends his family to live with a married son, and disappears over the mountain to suffer alone the price he has paid in expiating Jerry's evil.

The spartan character of Ebenezer Straint and the mystical overtones of the story place "Brothers of No Kin" a decided cut above the other early stories. In fact, both Ebenezer and Jeremiah Ritter, the latter unique by reason of his insidious nature, surpass all other male characterizations in the collected volume, as well as in the uncollected works of the first two decades. Through Ebenezer's altruistic act for Jeremiah—his assumption of guilt—the story affiliates itself thematically with *The Sea of Grass, Tacey Cromwell,* and *The Fields.* By virtue of their promoting the theme of the assumption of guilt, all four works, in turn bespeak the mystical elements in Richter's philosophy.

In depicting the characters in "Brothers of No Kin," especially that of Ebenezer Straint, Richter demonstrates what became a hallmark of his writing: the faithful rendering of native speech. In this case, Ebenezer realistically employs the reserved and simple language of rural Pennsylvanians of the time, language ordinarily punctuated with biblical phraseology. Witness Ebenezer's prayer: "Give Thou to him what is mine, O Lord, my portion, my crown and passage to Heaven, and I take the sins of Jeremiah Ritter on my own head."[1] The directness and economy of Richter's writing style stands in marked contrast to, say, that of James Fenimore Cooper, whose works Richter said he was never able to read.

Finally, "Brothers of No Kin" illustrates the early tendency of Richter to affix symbolic names to his characters. Ebenezer is from the Old Testament (1 Sam. 7:12) name meaning a memorial stone commemorating divine assistance. Jeremiah is from the prophet known for denunciation and judgment, both of which apply to the fictional character guilty of uncounted evils. In other stories in *Brothers of No Kin,* Robert Sturge ("The Laughter of Leen") is reminiscent of the sturgeon, a tough-bodied fish. Valentine Pierce, Jr. ("Forest Mould"), recalls the human heart associated with his first name, although initially he lacks true compassion. The last name of Theodora Pilgrim ("Wings of a Swallow") suggests the visionary qualities of the young woman in love with love. And Roger Bankson ("The Sure Thing") brings to mind the bank by which he is employed.

With the possible exception of "The Laughter of Leen," the other stories in *Brothers of No Kin,* as well as the uncollected ones of this period, are undistinguished. And from the standpoint of plot alone "The Laughter of Leen" would hardly merit consideration. Thaleen (Leen) Juste applies for a position as governess in the household of a Mrs. Margaret Brookins. When she refuses to promise that she will not discipline Mrs. Brookins's spoiled son Robert, Leen is ordered to leave. But at this point Mrs. Brookins's brother Robert Sturge intervenes and persuades his sister to reconsider. Leen's laughter infects the household and changes everything for the better, including little Robert's conduct and Mrs. Brookins's disposition. Only Sturge seems relatively unimpressed. One evening, when Leen's laughter interferes with a business transaction of his, he admonishes her to control herself. Leen says that if she cannot laugh, she cannot bear life; later she explains to Sturge that she has lost her father, mother, and brother in the war (World War I) that also destroyed her home. Sturge offers to send Leen back to help rehabilitate her native Belgium. But, because he loves her and she him, Leen elects to remain in America.

"The Laughter of Leen," despite external appearances, actually avoids sentimentality and instead turns more toward pathos under Richter's finely muted style. But even then it would deserve little attention were it not that in the character Leen, it anticipates the virtues of the Richter heroine that come to flower in Sayward Luckett Wheeler of the historical trilogy. In this respect, "The Laughter of Leen" invites comparison with another story in *Brothers of No Kin*. "Wings of a Swallow" imbues the character Theodora Pilgrim with similar traits of honesty, strength of character, perseverance, and adaptability.

Through its heroine, "The Laughter of Leen" becomes the first of several works of fiction by Richter to make a plea for brotherhood and human understanding. Thaleen Juste has lost parents and brother in Belgium during World War I. Rather than embittering her toward the Germans, however, the experience prompts her to plead for understanding of them: "The men of one army—they think they do right like the men of the other think! The men of one die and suffer like the men of the other. The women of the Germans lose the men they love so much as we Belgians, so much as the French. Oh! What matter if it German, if it French or Belgian is?"[2] In thus promoting the theme of brotherhood, "The Laughter of Leen" links itself with such successors as the short story "Good Neighbors" (*Saturday Evening Post,* 30 October 1943) and the novels *Tacey Cromwell* (1942) and *The Light in the Forest* (1953).

Inherent in the plot of "The Laughter of Leen," as in the earlier "How Tuck Went Home," is a second theme of altruism, which grows out of Leen's selfless service to the Brookins family. Altruism, like brotherhood, is a theme that sums up the essence of Richter's philosophical theories of evolutionary progress. And when one considers that

Leen Juste's last name may well have been inspired by the French term *juste-milieu,* (the golden mean in human relations), the idea assumes larger dimension.

Just as Richter's theories of human energy supply and expenditure help explain his preference for certain themes, they illuminate facets of characterization. According to the philosophical works, for example, excessive energy expenditure may create a vacuum in the human organism, which then must employ a relief process to correct the imbalance. Such a vacuum frequently occurs because of the death of a "loved one," thoughts of whom send an individual's cellular vibration rate flaring up "instantly, commanded by association with the dread intruder [death]." To correct the imbalance, the individual's own organism "blindly throws an additional force of energy against the mental opposition."[3] Moreover, the therapeutic "additional force" often is laughter, which Richter defines as a "physical method of spending the surplus energy suddenly formed by an abrupt drop in vibration rate below full energy flow stage."[4] In "The Laughter of Leen," the heroine has lost her parents and brother. Inferentially, then, the thought of their deaths sends her cellular vibration rate soaring; and, to correct the imbalance, she laughs. Viewed in this wise, her laughter becomes meaningful. Otherwise, it would have to be considered almost maniacal.

The other ten stories in *Brothers of No Kin* have been appraised even by Richter himself as the products of "a young married man intent on getting a bit of magazine money for his small family."[5] A similar evaluation would be appropriate for the uncollected stories of this period.

For settings in all these early works, Richter usually employs his own rural or urban Pennsylvania. An exception not previously mentioned is New York in which portions of "Tempered Copper" and "The Old Debt" are set. For plots, the author resorts entirely to the melodramatic, with trick endings reminiscent of O. Henry. Virtually all of the stories have happy endings, one of which constitutes a reverse twist of that of the title story in the collected volume. In "Brothers of No Kin" an indigent returns home for assistance from a wealthy friend. But in "Rich Relations" (*American,* March 1924) the reverse is the case.

A synoptic summary of the remaining stories in *Brothers of No Kin* suggests the basic weaknesses of Richter's early plots. "Forest Mould" portrays a spoiled young man, whose father devises a faked-murder scheme to send the son fleeing to the country, where hard work in a sawmill makes a man of him. A similar scheme, sans the melodrama of a pretended crime, regenerates the hero in "Tempered Copper." In

"Wings of a Swallow" a woman, whose romantic dreams suffer setback on confrontation by the reality of a hardhearted employer, is rescued by an enterprising young man's turning the tables on his fiancée's superior and then winning a job for himself from the same employer. A wealthy father, pretending financial ruin, in "Over the Hill to the Rich House," makes wholesome persons out of a spoiled wife and son forced to work for a change. The "Suicide," a young man who has stolen money from his employer, loses himself (hence the title) on a lonely farm long enough to gain physical vigor, self-respect, and the forgiveness of the employer's daughter. "Smokehouse" features a farmer who outmaneuvers a crooked speculator and thus convinces a city girl, formerly employed by the speculator before moving to the country in search of health, that the simple life is the best. Similarly, in "The Sure Thing," a conservative young man saves his elder's money by secretly depositing it in a bank's savings account rather than investing it as directed in a mining venture that fails. Another young banker, in "Bad Luck is Good Luck," acquires self-reliance when compelled by his employer's pretended illness and consequent absence to assume control of the business. In "Swanson's 'Home Sweet Home,'" a railroad engineer, with an obsession for playing "Home Sweet Home" on his engine whistle, does a good turn for a lady in distress and is rewarded with her hand in marriage.

For characters, as the foregoing synopses imply, Richter ordinarily marshals such stereotypes as a wise old head, a promising but petulant young charge, and a virtuous heroine who assists the old head in regenerating the hero. As an added attraction in such stories as "Forest Mould" and "Suicide," the author introduces a poor but deserving youth who also helps bring out the nobler side of the hero and who, in turn, is financially rewarded for his rehabilitation efforts.

As though reacting to the licentiousness and cynicism of the Roaring Twenties, these stories thematically promote the concept of what Richter calls "hardship-into-gain." Such a process requires self-discipline, which, as Richter's philosophical works insist, is conducive to the production of human energy. In earlier times, Richter said, people "had to walk, work, struggle long hours." Such hardship made a man "stronger, gave him endurance, resourcefulness, built up his independence, pride in self-reliance."[6] Today, however, Richter believed, Americans had acquired such ease and luxury that they had become "easy, soft."

In another context—an aside in the short story "Bad Luck Is Good Luck"—Richter approaches self-discipline in terms of "agony" and again harks back to his philosophical theories of cellular vibration: "There are few greater stimuli to action than agony. Agony accomplishes either miracles or murder, rolls away mountains or commits suicide. It is the divine rheostat at which the mortal battery is charged with storage power to feed the divine spark to the human cylinders."[7]

To reinforce the concept of hardship-into-gain, Richter introduces into some of his early stories another theme bearing on the opposite side of the coin. Appearing especially in "Forest Mould" and "Over the Hill to the Rich House," it is the detrimental effects of overly indulgent parents on the offspring.

The glorification of hard work and the deprecation of easy gain Richter accomplishes by juxtaposing rural life and urban in such a way as to idealize the farm. On the subconscious and mystical levels, the result is an idyll of the farm. This familiar agrarian myth is a corollary of the larger theme of the organic unity of humans and nature, which, in turn, ties to Richter's philosophical theory that all life and matter are governed by natural laws.

On the level of physical action in the stories, the theme of organic unity is presented indirectly through the portrayal of young men, with no previous contact with the land, who are suddenly thrust upon the farm or into the woods and who acquire a love for nature. The theme is more nearly evident here, however, in the relationship of humans and nature's creatures, such as a dog in "The Man Who Loved a Hound" (*Elks Magazine*, December 1925) and birds in "Smokehouse." This is made clear in the following rustic Emersonian declaration by the character Tully, in "Smokehouse":

They'll [birds will] talk to you first time they see you, which is more'n most folks in the city will do. The fire bird'll set right down on the pasture bars under your nose and show off his red vest like a model in a big store, and ask what you think of it plain as whippoorwill. Of course, they all don't exactly talk with their mouths. The Lord give us various languages. But it don't take no dictionary and grammar book to learn. All you got to get on to is listening with your eyes, and you can even visit with the trees.[8]

The melodramatic plots, type characters, and conventional themes prompt one to agree with Bruce Sutherland's estimate that Richter's early efforts are mainly "stories tailored for the trade." But this judgment does not mean that the works may be completely ignored. They presage the authorial technique of relying upon personal materials and, consequently, are somewhat necessary orientation to the later, more successful works. Further strengthening this impression is "The Old Debt," most autobiographical of the early stories, which might well have been an episode in *A Simple Honorable Man*. In fact, the ice-cream parlor scene from the story actually does appear in the later novel. Still other parallels are a minister's family, which in both story and novel consists of three sons resembling Richter and his own two brothers; and an eldest son (Richter himself), who (1) as a child tries to run away to the West and (2) as a young man works for Westinghouse in Pittsburgh.

These early stories promote elemental virtues, which, under more sophisticated treatment, would make much of Richter's fiction a paean to goodness; and, more important, they relate to various facets of his theories of human energy supply and expenditure and hence contribute to the thematic unity of the corpus of his fiction. Finally, the early stories maintain the consistency of tone, the clarity of style, and the concision of presentation that, under even further refinement, became the hallmarks of Richter's art.

Chapter Four
Westering

Conrad Richter's literary career reached a turning point in 1928, when circumstances resembling a chapter from his early fiction brought personal reversal that, paradoxically, proved fortunate. Primarily responsible for that turn of events, the serious illness of Richter's wife prompted the family to leave Pennsylvania for a more favorable climate. Richter sold his farm in Clarks Valley, disposed of his business holdings, and moved reluctantly to New Mexico. A land of ethnical and geographical contradictions, farther removed than the two thousand miles that actually separated it from the East, Albuquerque and environs nevertheless aroused immediately in the new arrivals what Richter later described as a "phenomenon in sensation." The Richters found that "simple quiet scenes such as a green lombardy against an adobe house" imbued them with "a vitality of feeling not to be found elsewhere."[1]

But if such "scenes" were therapeutic for Richter's wife, they were disturbing to his fictional habits. The characters and plots of the highly civilized area with which he had been concerned were incompatible to a land still largely a frontier in the twentieth century. Casting about for fresh materials, therefore, Richter relied upon the technique of personal experience that he had utilized during the first two decades of his writing. From childhood he had heard stories of the West from relatives living there. To this storehouse he added information gleaned from "the yellow files of newspapers printed on paper hauled across the great plains on ox trains, and the rare books, manuscripts, and personal records left by the early adventurers and settlers of both sexes."[2] Of Richter's exhaustive research work in the Southwest, T. M. Pearce says, "When I first knew him, he was filling his notebooks with data about the pioneer West, data that was to come forth recreated as the flesh and blood of Frank and Nettie Gant in 'Smoke over the Prairie' or as the rugged Jim Brewton and his lovely wife Lutie in *The Sea of Grass*. Something of the 'flavor' of the notebooks hangs over *Early Americana*, but in *The Sea of Grass* authentic details, pulsing thought, and strong emotion flow together with the substance of reality."[3]

In addition to materials he acquired from documents, interviews with persons having firsthand experience in earlier events provided Richter with fictional materials. Some of those persons were his Albuquerque neighbors: a geologist, who knew the history of the mines, and his wife, who knew the history of the mine people; a retired rancher; and a Mexican husband and wife, the latter "the daughter of a Mazatlan ship building family and a Scotch sea captain."[4] From the geologist and his wife, Richter acquired background materials for his novel *Tacey Cromwell,* which is set in a mining town. Qualities suggested by the Mexican-born wife figured into Richter's novel *The Lady,* whose protagonist is a woman of mixed Mexican and English ancestry.

The couple that provided Richter with his finest southwestern background materials lived near his house in Albuquerque. They were Herbert and Lou Hardy, who had lived in New Mexico in the days before it gained statehood. The hallway of their house "hung with long horns and oldtime photographs."[5]

Not all of Richter's living sources proved as helpful as the Hardys. Richter recalled a man that had been a companion of a "famous early character." When he asked the source about his companion, Richter said, all the information he received about an "exciting human being" was that the man "was about five-feet-eight, dark complected and weighed around a hundred and sixty pounds."[6]

If some persons he sought out proved less than satisfactory sources, however, others who approached Richter were surprisingly rewarding. One of those, Isabel McAtee Dow, had been introduced to Richter by her son, who drove a laundry truck serving the Richters. Mrs. Dow had known Billy the Kid. When Richter interviewed her, he found that her stories about the Kid left him "cold" but that her accounts of her own life in frontier New Mexico in the 1860s appealed to him very much. One such account concerned the trips that Richter's informant and her young brother took unaccompanied to Santa Fe for supplies. The trip required several days and took the youngsters through Apache Indian country.[7] Material obtained from Mrs. Dow informs Richter's story "Early Marriage" and other works.

Even a cursory examination of the materials gleaned from written and oral sources convinced Richter of the striking parallel between the New Mexico of the late nineteenth century and the Allegheny frontier of the late eighteenth. The two regions might differ to the senses, but they corresponded in the demands they made upon pioneers. Having moved two thousand miles away, Richter thus found himself inhabiting the backgrounds of both East and Southwest, and, in each instance, viewing a vanished past. By 1933, five years after undertaking his quest for new materials in his adopted region, he had reached two significant decisions: (1) that his earlier attitude toward writing as a means merely of earning money had been wrong, a wrong he would now attempt to right by producing the best fiction of which he was capable, and (2) that historical fiction offered the best promise.

In deciding to write historical fiction, Richter perhaps recognized that a disturbing situation in modern American life was the ignorance of native backgrounds and history. If so, he perhaps realized further that the failure resulted largely from literary trends of the 1920s and 1930s. The gay cynicism of the Roaring Twenties had become a resentful and bitter pessimism during the depression. With the stock market collapse 24 October 1929, the Charleston lines had become bread lines, and a new social consciousness—indeed, a social protest—had become pronounced in national letters. Such a preoccupation of writers had produced a shift in emphasis from the past to the present and to the future. Even writers who had not ignored the past tended often to misunderstand it. In short, Richter may have realized that much contemporary historical fiction amounted to nothing more than escapism for readers desperately seeking relief from the complexities of industrial society and from the tribulations of economic reversals. As such, literature might provide entertainment; but it could not—in Bruce Sutherland's words—"integrate the past and the present in terms of moral values, human relationships, and the 'fulness' of life."[8]

On the other hand, properly depicted, pioneer fortitude could be employed in such a way as to bring frustrated contemporaries into closer contact with people of another age—people who also lived, loved, struggled, and died, but whose lives nevertheless reflected purpose, completeness, and serenity. "The fight for freedom, dignity, self-respect, and security occurs in every generation," Sutherland correctly asserts. "Conditions change but the goal for which man strives remains the same, and sometimes out of the past comes a clearer vision of that goal than can be seen in the obscurity of a muddied present and a clouded future."[9] Richter was aware of this verity, that the growth of American culture is dependent upon the past, as well as the present, and that the will to survive in the present is often inspired by the examples of the past.

The resolve to write quality fiction, however, was not so easily made as the decision to concentrate on historical subjects. Mounting medical expenses of his wife and the steadily diminishing market for fiction in the depression had brought Richter perilously near to financial collapse. "Mrs. Richter's sister, a nurse, had moved to Albuquerque to help care for my wife," Richter recalls. "One Christmas, when she gave us a small amount of money, we rejoiced as though it were a fortune. It was the first ready cash we had had in days."[10] The wonder, then, is that the author successfully avoided concentrating entirely on the popular stories with which he had been reasonably successful financially the first twenty years of his literary career.

Early Americana

Nevertheless, Richter did continue to write often for the popular magazines, including the pulps. By the time his first collection of southwestern stories had been published as *Early Americana* (1936), all nine of the works had appeared previously either in the *Saturday Evening Post* or in *Ladies' Home Journal*. The difference was that, by this time, Richter had learned he could produce quality works that would sell.

With the publication of *Early Americana,* Richter's fourth book-length work, a chorus of critical acclaim sounded for the first really discernible time. "It must be a careless reader," wrote novelist Charles J. Finger, "who fails to realize that here is an admirably trained intellect with fine perception of character reproducing impressions of life; not the life of today, but of a past neglected by historians and enshrined in forgotten newspapers."[11] To Stanley Young, the frontier under Richter's "eye becomes not the drab, dreary scene of drudgery that the realism of a Garland would give"; indeed, Richter succeeds better than Harte in creating an "impression of unity in the life that is just behind us."[12]

The stories in *Early Americana*, by Richter's stated intention, seek to portray the "small authenticities" of daily life—but not of history per se—"without which life would not be life either then or today," and to do so "in a style suggestive of those times that are gone but not dead." Such a time was the frontier period of the post–Civil War nineteenth century, and such places were Independence, the Santa Fe trail, Taos, Bent's Fort, and Santa Fe—the Staked Plains, or Llano Estacado, of New Mexico and Texas. Border raids, Indian uprisings, the arrival of homesteaders, and the feuds of stockmen and nesters constitute the plots, which, for the most part, are simple episodes.

"Early Marriage" depicts the narrow escape from Indian massacre of a young woman journeying from her father's isolated trading post to wed her fiancé. "Long Drouth," originally published as "Long Engagement" (*Saturday Evening Post,* 16 June 1934), recreates the life and death of the land during five rainless years that delay the marriage of the heroine. In "New Home" a homesteader leaves wife and infant exposed to forays by rival land seekers and Indians, while he is gone for a fortnight to legalize his land claim. "Frontier Woman," somewhat like "Early Marriage," describes the tribulations of a mother and daughter migrating in the aftermath of the Civil War from Georgia to New Mexico. A feud between cattlemen erupts in "The Square Piano," almost spoiling the debut of the first piano in a frontier community and nearly costing the life of a young rancher whose betrothal is cemented after he is wounded. "Buckskin Vacation" portrays a rancher's daughter, home on holiday from a female seminary in Missouri, who succeeds in a secret wedding to a young army officer. The clash between the old way (represented by Frank Gant, a rancher) and the new (symbolized by the railroad) takes place in "Smoke over the Prairie." In "As It Was in the Beginning," a Santa Fe trader, seeking a wife, bargains for a white girl captive of the Comanches; and, when the intended bride protests the arrangement, he then wins her consent in courtship. "Early Americana," the title piece, revolves around a young couple married at a frontier post after the principals in another wedding set for the same place have been killed by Indians.

Short, succinct, and uncluttered, these stories never evidence interest in documentation for its own sake. Authentic details exist, yes, but they never intrude because of Richter's restraint, selectivity, and tight narrative structure. Suggested rather than emphasized are the scenes in which atmosphere takes precedence over a specific canvas. Emotions remain taut and strong impressions of passion and danger persist, yet the stories are not without flashes of humor. Richter's humor characteristically is quiet, as in the simile in "Early Americana" that Mr. and Mrs. Oldham's breathing is "like the hoofbeats of Ben and Fanny," their saddle horses, or in still another simile, from the same story, that Judge Tatum is a long figure "with a face like a sorrel horse." The style is clear, supple, colloquial, punctuated with figures of frontier speech in its phrasing. In short, proceeding "somewhat like an impressionistic painter," to employ John T. Flanagan's apt phrase, "Richter employs bright and challenging colors but concentrates more on mood and tone than on unblurred outline."[13]

Although violence enters into most of the tales, it is ordinarily shorn of much of the actual brutality. More discernibly than Faulkner, who contended that he avoided sensationalism for its own sake, Richter actually mutes killings and mutilations by suggesting, rather than detailing, them. In "Early Americana," for example, the intended bride Nellie Hedd, her fiancé, and her family are massacred by Indians. Depicting the discovery of the bodies by young Laban Oldham, the author relegates the sordid aspects to a fade-out: Laban "had made out a feather shaft like a long, thin, uplifted finger warning him grimly not to come on. And now for the first time he knew the naked and mutilated object on the buckboard tongue for what it was."[14]

The emphasis often is the land itself and its challenge that is a siren call to the pioneers. Here are desert and mesa, arroyo and peak—a hard land, arid and rocky, and one in which people grapple not only nature, but others for their very existence. To endure and prevail, then, they must possess those qualities that Richter promotes in his philosophical writing about human energy supply and expenditure: self-discipline, determination, vigor, pride. Such virtues are markedly evident in Richter's characters—authentic mountain men, soldiers, ranchers, Indians, and homesteaders, some of whom, such as Ceran St. Vrain and William Bent, are even drawn from actual life.

For example, "Early Marriage," published first in the 7 April 1934 issue of the *Saturday Evening Post,* introduces Richter's first distinctive Western hero. Asa Putman, a rugged individualist, has triumphed by surviving the hardships of his frontier trading post; in turn, he has succeeded also by imbuing in his daughter Nancy Belle qualities essential to her successful journey through hostile Indian country to her wedding. Although sketchily drawn, Putman appears in sufficient relief to prepare the way for later men and women of his breed not only in Richter's western fiction but in his Ohio trilogy.

The same bequeathal by a father to a daughter of the pioneer qualities necessary for survival against any hardship recurs in "Long Drouth." In it, however, the father (Sylvester Davis) is a horse rancher rather than a trader, and his daughter (Joanna) waits five patient years for her lover to come to her.

In Lalla Porterfield, the "Frontier Woman," Richter creates perhaps his strongest heroine in the short stories before 1936. Disillusioned by the loss of her plantation home and by the social station in the Civil War, she still refrains from cynicism; instead she confronts frontier life without flinching.

Nancy Belle Putman, Joanna Davis, Lalla Porterfield—Richter reveals them by providing little flashes of insight into their souls and by giving them perseverance and a stoical acceptance of conditions over which they have little control. Pioneer fortitude, of course, can be easily overdone; extreme realism is often a misrepresentation of life. But such pitfalls Richter avoids by refusing to portray these women as legendary heroines or as the victims of frontier neuroses. His chief concern is with ordinary women to whom the life is neither heroic nor lacklustre; it is a life that has to be lived, and, when material values fail, spiritual forces can be marshaled for sustenance.

That is not to say that *Early Americana* completely avoids some of the weaknesses of Richter's earlier stories. "The Square Piano," for example, suffers from a sentimental ending. And "Buckskin Vacation" fails to strike a proper balance between hardship and gain. In marked contrast, however, "New Home" and "Early Americana" achieve harmonious fusion of disaster and triumph, and they brilliantly capture the "actualities" of daily life in the early Southwest.

By depicting pioneers from the viewpoints of their motivations and their contacts with the land, elements, and mortal enemies, Richter introduces into *Early Americana* and the corpus of his fiction, themes and corollaries growing out of the processes of "westering." "Westering," in turn, connects to Richter's theories of human energy supply and expenditure. Helpful to an understanding of this thematic technique is a review of the historian Frederick Jackson Turner's hypothesis that insists that the frontier has been the one great determinant of American civilization. The existence of an area of free land, its continuous recession, and the advance of American settlement westward molded the national character. The frontier promoted a composite American nationality, decreased the nation's dependence on England, determined the growth of nationalism and the evolution of political institutions, transformed the democracy of Jefferson into the national republicanism of Monroe and the democracy of Jackson, and promoted democracy here and in Europe. But if, in this westward march, men and women transformed the frontier, they in turn, were transformed by it, acquiring such traits (attributable to the frontier) as coarseness and strength; acuteness and acquisitiveness; a practical, inventive turn of mind quick to find expedients; a masterful grasp of material things, lacking in the artistic but powerful to effect great changes; restless and nervous energy; and a dominant individualism, working for good and evil.

The frontiers Turner saw as being the fall line of the seventeenth century, the Alleghenies of the eighteenth, and the Mississippi and Missouri rivers and the Rocky Mountains of the nineteenth. But, regardless of the frontier, the waves of advancement were similar. First came the pioneers, living on natural vegetation and clearing the land. In their wake came groups that purchased land, added more, and built permanent settlements. Finally came capital and enterprise.

But what, one might ask, prompted these waves of American civilization? On the physical and conscious levels, the answer, according to Turner, is the pursuit of material gain and the desire to escape the confines of civilization, including laws. Such motives are inherent in the actions of all of Richter's characters, whose arrival on the frontier illustrates the theme of restless wandering. And this theme, in turn, is suggestive of "inharmony," which results from the lean supply and excessive expenditure of human energy and which is best satisfied by physical exertion such as moving about or working. Restless wandering is evident in "Long Drouth," in the full-scale migration of ranchers from New Mexico to South Dakota; in "Early Marriage," in the lonely trek of a young woman and her brother to meet her intended bridegroom; in "New Home" and "Frontier Woman," in the arduous travel of women seeking new starts in life in the West; in "Smoke over the Prairie," in the wagon trains of farmers searching for new land; and in "Early Americana," in the activity of buffalo hunters who constantly follow the trail of game.

Emerging from the late frontier and early community stages of the processes of "westering" are the themes and corollaries of people enduring and prevailing. Such concepts of a positive nature illustrate Richter's theories of evolutionary progress. The foremost theme in this category—hardship-into-gain—has a counterpart in Richter's early fiction unrelated to "westering," but in the later work it is demonstrated in "New Home" by the young mother who holds her home against marauding cowboys and Indians until her husband can return from legalizing the claim to their homestead; in "Early Marriage," "Long Drouth," "The Square Piano," "Buckskin Vacation," "Smoke over the Prairie," "As It Was in the Beginning," and "Early Americana" by young women who overcome obstacles to their marriage; and in "Frontier Woman" by a Southern belle, deprived of home and position, who finds both again in the West. These characters experiencing hardship-into-gain have kinship with those in the earlier, non-"westering" stories: "Forest Mould," "Suicide," "Bad Luck Is Good Luck," and "Tempered Copper."

Richter well knows, of course, that people did not always endure and prevail in the course of "westering." For this reason, he introduces into these stories several corollaries of a negative nature. The theme of the tragedy of youthful death, for example, is presented in "Early Americana" through the massacre by Indians of the intended bride and bridegroom, Nellie Hedd and Jack Shelby. And in "New Home," the plight of a young mother left alone, except for her infant child, while her husband goes to secure their homestead claim, and, in "Early Americana," the long vigil of a teenage girl in the hushed expectancy of an Indian attack—both of these illustrate the theme of loneliness. The theme is reinforced through the musing of the character Laban Oldham, who tells himself that white women "didn't belong out here. Their place was back in a gentler land where farmers never heard of turning a furrow with a rifle lashed to the plow handles and where, on a Sunday morning, his mother used to say, she could still remember the peaceful sound of church bells drifting across the blue-grass."[15]

Again, from the late frontier and early community stages of "westering" in these stories come the themes and corollaries of historical change. The theme of the old way in conflict with the new is demonstrated in "Smoke over the Prairie" by the rancher Frank Gant's fight with the railroad. Mixed marriages of Anglo-Americans and either Mexicans or Indians, as revealed in "As It Was in the Beginning," suggest the theme of America as an ethnic melting pot. The mixed allegiance of a person to two opposing ethnic groups is a theme evident in the character Ursula Ross, who, in "As It Was in the Beginning," is an Anglo-American woman captive of Indians. Finally, the theme of the duality of civilization, which is at once good and evil, is posed in "Smoke over the Prairie," which forecasts the destruction of grass lands by imprudent farmers.

On the subconscious and mystical levels, the processes of "westering" encourage two themes in *Early Americana*. The rite de passage, the mythical initiation of an individual into some phase of life, is illustrated in "Early Americana" by the induction into manhood of the youthful hero Laban Oldham and into womanhood by the equally youthful heroine Chatherine Minor. An even more mystical theme also grows out of the characterization of Laban Oldham. He desires to leave his father's home for "a free life, a king's life, with always a new camp and a new country just over the rise"—to leave and never to "come back to sleep again in a house at Carnuel."[16] To understand the theme inherent here, one might recall that, in assaying motives for seeking out the American frontier, D. H. Lawrence suggests that the dominant reason was not so much material gain as it was to "get away"—away from everything one is and has been. But, if people were prompted to seek the frontier to "get away" from everything, they found ultimately that they had unwittingly imprisoned themselves. In other words, they discovered that they cannot be free away from those things they sought to avoid. Lawrence makes this point as follows: "Men are free when they are in a living homeland, not when they are straying and breaking away. Men are free when they are obeying some deep, inward voice of religious belief. Obeying from within. Men are free when they belong to a living, organic, *believing* community, active in fulfilling some unfulfilled, perhaps unrealized purpose. Not when they are escaping to some wild west. Men are freest when they are most unconscious of freedom."[17]

That is to say people are free only when they are doing what the "deepest self" (the inner self) likes. Conversely, they are not free when they are doing merely what the surface self likes. This clash between the inner and surface selves produces a higher manifestation of what Richter calls "in-harmony"—a dissatisfaction resulting from energy hunger that here takes the form of a subconscious alienation from both the earthly and the Spiritual father, the former of whom is a symbol of the latter.

In the longings of Laban Oldham to leave his father's house are tentative signs of an alienation from his earthly (and hence his Spiritual) father. The gulf, however, does not become so pronounced here as elsewhere in Richter's fiction, for adversity (the antidote to "inharmony") gives Oldham a deeper understanding of his earthly father. But if Laban Oldham does not become alienated from his earthly and Spiritual fathers, his successors do. *The Sea of Grass, The Town, The Lady, The Light in the Forest,* and *A Country of Strangers,* among Richter's historical works, and "The Old Debt," *The Waters of Kronos,* and *A Simple Honorable Man,* among his nonhistorical, all explore the mystical theme of alienation and reconciliation.

Like the eastern stories Richter wrote early in his career, *Early Americana* tales often deal with the theme of the organic unity of humans and nature. The eastern stories, however, examine the relationship in modern or civilized times and ordinarily focus upon a spoiled young man whose encounter with a farm or the forest improves his character. On the other hand, the southwestern stories are set during frontier days, when facilities were limited and the natural challenges therefore much more difficult. Southwestern people, in other words, as Richter says in an essay, find the "land hard to love and so loved the more."

In *Brothers of No Kin,* Richter often promotes the agrarian myth. His *Early Americana* stories continue the practice except that they alter the idyll of the farm to the mystique of the wilderness. A typical example may be found in the title story of the southwestern collection in which the speaker imagines a night long ago on the Staked Plains, "with no light but the ancient horns of the Comanche moon and that milky band of star dust stirred up by the passing of some celestial herd."[18]

In revealing the character Sylvester Davis's (and his daughter Joanna's) deep attraction to horses, "Long Drouth" reinforces the theme of organic unity and also relates itself to an earlier story of the close bond between humans and one of nature's creatures, "The Man Who Loved A Hound." But since nature's side of the organic relationship is ambivalent, "Long Drouth," as its title suggests, also illustrates the negative corollary theme of the life and death of the land. The scene reinforcing this corollary theme is stark: "of skies black with crows, of the few remaining water-holes reeking with dead cattle, of . . . mares eating mistletoe from the junipers and losing their colts from the ergot, of wells and springs going dry through the Panhandle and Arizona territory, and settlers forced to move."[19]

The Sea of Grass

In 1937, two decades after his short works of fiction had begun appearing, the publication of *The Sea of Grass* won Conrad Richter immediate acclaim indeed remarkable for a first novel. Praised for having "immensely subtilized and sophisticated the types and themes of the better Western novel,"[20] Richter also reaped financial reward.[21] The novel quickly sold fifteen thousand copies and then was purchased for a motion picture featuring Spencer Tracy and Katherine Hepburn.[22]

Before appearing in book form, *The Sea of Grass* had run serially in the *Saturday Evening Post* 31 October and 7 and 14 November 1936. In this respect it anticipated a publishing pattern to be repeated by Richter with four other novels. *The Free Man* (1943), *Always Young and Fair* (1947), *The Light in the Forest* (1953), and *The Lady* (1957) likewise would appear serially in the *Saturday Evening Post* before they did in book form.

The success enjoyed by *The Sea of Grass* is reminiscent of that of another first novel, *The Time of Man,* whose author, Elizabeth Madox Roberts, invites comparison in several ways with Conrad Richter. At the time of the publication of her novel in 1926, Roberts was forty-five years of age, two years younger than Richter at the time of the publication of *The Sea of Grass.* Then, like Roberts's, Richter's novel grows out of the life of a place and is told in a language firmly rooted in that place. Finally, both writers work with such materials as idiom, folk tales, and folk superstitions.

The success of *The Sea of Grass* also raises the question of why Richter had not undertaken earlier to write a novel. Certainly, as his notebooks indicate, his exhaustive research in New Mexico (and earlier in Pennsylvania, as his subsequent eastern American historical novels would show)—his research had unearthed much information requiring more detailed treatment than shorter forms of fiction permit. Nevertheless, Richter had to assimilate that mass of material, a process through which he doubtless was going while writing the *Early Americana* stories (and through which he would go in writing eastern American historical short stories before publishing his Pennsylvania-Ohio historical trilogy of novels in the 1940s and early 1950s). Moreover, by temperament and experience, he felt more at ease with carefully constructed, condensed stories than with the long, padded epic typical of American historical writing; he strived to find a different vehicle that would meet both the expectations of his organic theory of composition and the sheer weight of his materials. Obviously he found the proper vehicle, but, before he did, like the producer of rare wine, Richter refused to release his novel before its time.

Then, when he did release his novel, Richter still appeared to do so almost grudgingly. In outline *The Sea of Grass* posed highly theatrical material that could easily verge on melodrama. Richter recognized that possibility and compensated by determining on a brief and restrained, almost taciturn, approach. Furthermore, the unity of impression Richter considered crucial to the work argued against the long novel, just as it did the long short story. For those reasons, Richter chose the novella form.

The idea for *The Sea of Grass* was not exactly new to Richter. He had explored some facets of the plot in his short story "Smoke over the Prairie," first published in the 1 June 1935 issue of the *Saturday Evening Post* and then collected in *Early Americana.* As in the short story but not in the other stories of *Early Americana,* Indians in *The*

Sea of Grass no longer are the villains. Instead, the plot turns on the classical feud between ranchers, who would preserve the sea of grass for their cattle, and farmers, who would plow up the grassland to make way for their crops. Nature also plays a prominent role, sending winds that swirl the soil foolishly plowed and withholding the rainfall necessary for the growing of wheat and corn.

Against such a backdrop in New Mexico during the last two decades of the nineteenth century the story unfolds, told twenty-five years after it has ended by Hal Brewton, the interested but detached nephew of the principal character, Colonel James Brewton. Jim Brewton is a legendary cattle baron whose Cross B Ranch and adjacent free range are "larger than Massachusetts with Connecticut thrown in." It spreads about 120 miles north to south along the Rio Grande from approximately Santo Domingo to Socorro and then westward to the Arizona line. The day that the colonel's betrothed, Lutie Cameron, arrives in Salt Fork, two of Colonel Brewton's cowhands, who had shot at a nester on Cross B free range, are being exonerated by a jury of ranchers. Brice Chamberlain, lawyer for the nester, protests that the colonel's victory will not be permanent. But if Jim Brewton is content with his power and his life, his wife Lutie resents the loneliness and dullness. A vivacious Saint Louis belle, anachronistic to the southwestern frontier, she is reminiscent of the heroine of Dorothy Scarborough's novel *The Wind.*

In a desperate effort to combat what she considers to be the drabness of ranch life, Lutie Brewton fills the house with furniture and flowers and has planted about it rows of cottonwoods and tamarisks. To her numerous parties flock guests from the whole territory—officers from the army posts, neighboring ranchers, officials of the railroad companies, and Brice Chamberlain, who becomes Lutie's favorite dancing partner. Friends of Colonel Brewton hope that Lutie will settle down after the birth of her three children, a daughter (Sarah Beth) and two sons (Jimmy and Brock). But their whispered speculation that the second son, Brock, has been fathered not by Jim Brewton but by Brice Chamberlain—gossip Colonel Brewton at least outwardly ignores[23]—foreshadows Lutie's decision to flee New Mexico. "I'm going where there's life," she asserts desperately. "I'm going to balls and theaters and shaded streets and up-to-date stores and where every day people drive in the parks!"[24] Departing, Lutie leaves her children with her husband and his Negro servant, Black Hetty, a character inspired by an actual freed woman of the same name who had nursed Conrad Richter as an infant.

Fifteen years elapse. During this time a change in national political administrations establishes Brice Chamberlain as the territorial judge and thus prepares the way for an invasion of farmers into the free range. Meanwhile, Hal Brewton has become a medical doctor in Salt Fork, and the three children of the colonel have grown up. Brock, terribly spoiled by Colonel Brewton who seems intent on proving he has no doubt that the boy is his son, has taken to drinking, gambling, and barroom brawling. He shoots and kills Dutch Charley, a gambler, and then turns outlaw, simultaneously changing his name from Brewton to Chamberlain.

The day that Brock is killed by a posse, Lutie returns unannounced and without explanation for her absence. Superficially at least, she is accepted by the colonel; but to those outside the household, including the nephew Hal and the two remaining children, it is never clear how complete the reconciliation is. The feud between rancher and nester has been settled by a hostile nature that crushes the abortive farmer in the vise of its drought, and the story ends quietly.

Richter's handling of plot and character reveals for the first notable time his preference for a particular point of view. In *The Sea of Grass,* as in its shorter model, "Smoke over the Prairie," and in numerous works that followed, the author employs the middle-distance technique of a narrator youthful at the time of the action but mature at the time he relates the story as reminiscence. Such a point of view affords Richter the perspective dictated by the materials he has gleaned from oral sources and documents: he is approximately the same distance removed from the action as his narrator, Hal Brewton, at the time of the telling of the story. Moreover, the middle-distance narration provides both immediacy and historical perspective.

Hal Brewton, of course, is Richter; and, as such he reflects the author's own attitude toward his materials. Although not always objective, Hal relates the story with little moral comment, allowing his audience to judge for itself the action and the characters. His objectivity is due in part to his relationship to Colonel Brewton. He is sufficiently related to be interested in what happens to his uncle, but not so close as to have his vision blurred. Also, a doctor by the time he relates the story, he speaks with a sort of scientific objectivity. And in narrating the incidents years later, Hal understandably is able to mute the violence and sordidness, qualities repugnant to Richter. Finally, since Hal is frequently away from the scenes of action, he perforce deals exclusively with the highlights (the novel, like all of Richter's fiction, is episodic) and covers long periods of time with ease.

Such a point of view enables Richter, without sacrificing perspective or proportion, to pack into a few pages a quarter-century of historical change. This alteration—the passing of free range land—follows in the wake of the processes of "westering" from frontier to ranch to community. Like the stories in *Early Americana, The Sea of Grass* is set during a period that cuts across the frontier and community stages of "westering," and all of its themes (including historical change) grow out of these processes. On the physiological and conscious levels, for example, the theme of restless wandering is illustrated by the farmers who invade Jim Brewton's free-range land—men who have come West in search of a new start. These nesters thus relate themselves to those in the earlier story, "Smoke over the Prairie," which also contains the theme of restless wandering. Such wandering, in turn, connects to Richter's theory of "inharmony," a condition produced by the low supply and excessive expenditure of human energy, the antidote to which is physical exertion such as moving about or working.

A more prominent theme in *The Sea of Grass* is men and women enduring and prevailing, with its corollary of hardship-into-gain. Representative of those who have endured, prevailed, and gained from the hardship are the pioneer settlers, who, in Jim Brewton's words, "came out" to New Mexico and risked their lives and families "among the Indians" to establish ranches and towns. They are the antithesis of the nesters, who attempt to farm land unsuited for it, kill the grass that would sustain cattle, and demean themselves and their families.[25] By indirection, Brewton shows himself in his declaration to have been such a pioneer who endured and prevailed. His experience, according to Richter's philosophical theory of cellular energy supply and expenditure, is a mark of evolutionary progress.

But since people did not always prevail in the course of "westering," Richter realistically introduces into *The Sea of Grass* several negative corollaries that arise mainly from the lives of Lutie Brewton and her son Brock. Colonel Brewton and his nephew Hal love "that shaggy prairie," but Lutie hates it "passionately and secretly." And, in so doing, she illustrates the themes of loneliness and hardship of the frontier on women. Her hatred, of course, results in part from her refusal to adjust to primitive ways, a refusal that thus defeats her from the start. Foreshadowing and symbolizing this defeat, Lutie, upon disembarking from the train that has brought her from the East to New Mexico, throws away her bouquet of flowers as if to suggest that beauty could not exist in such a place. Her defeat anticipates a similar fate for the character Jary Luckett in *The Trees,* a novel also dealing with the theme of the inability of eastern woman to adjust to the frontier. The theme of the eager heart rejected finds expression in Lutie's abandonment by her paramour Brice Chamberlain, who she futilely believes will follow her into exile. Here she becomes linked with Tacey Cromwell, of the novel of the same name, who is failed by the man she loves.

Through Brock Brewton, Richter reveals the themes of the tragedy of youthful death and of the detriment of overly protective parents to a child. Brock's indulgence by Jim Brewton illustrates this latter theme. A similar theme had appeared in the earlier, non-"westering" stories, "Forest Mould" and "Over the Hill to the Rich House." Brock the first tragic character drawn by Richter, anticipates Rosa Tench of *The Town,* who is also illegitimate and driven to an early death. Both Brock and Rosa are strange and willful, and both suffer as if in expiation of the sins of their parents. In their suffering, the two are related to Seely Dowden of *Tacey Cromwell.*

The major theme growing out of the processes of "westering" is historical change. One of its corollaries is the conflict of the old way with the new, represented by the rancher-nester battle; this same concept is inherent in the earlier "Smoke over the Prairie." Out of the success of the farmers in obtaining free-range lands a second corollary develops: the duality of civilization that is at once good and evil. It is reinforced by the imprudent plowing up of grass and the futile efforts to farm land suited only for grazing. When a drought ensues, neither farmer nor rancher profits. The whole abortive experience marks a great historic change in the Southwest—the passing of free-range land.

Through the vehicle of Jim Brewton's strong attachment to his sea of grass the novel continues to explore the theme of the organic unity of humans and nature—a theme found earlier in *Early Americana* and *Brothers of No Kin.* Here, as in "Smoke over the Prairie" but unlike "Forest Mould" and its companion pieces of the twenties, the individual is already on the land rather than being thrust suddenly upon it. This means that he has had longer to appreciate the organic unity, and it also accounts for his affection, which takes on more mystical proportions. The result is a mystique of the wilderness, a theme carried over from *Early Americana* and one inherent in the musings of the narrator Hal Brewton: "The free wild life we lived on that shaggy prairie was to me the life of the gods. And that there should be anyone who would

not love it as we did, who should even hate it passionately and secretly
. . . had not occurred to me then."[26] Nature, however, is ambivalent,
and to demonstrate this verity the novel presents a negative corollary
of the theme of organic unity—the hostility of nature: the drought that
crushes the farmer and also injures the rancher.

On the subconscious and mystical levels, *The Sea of Grass* resumes
the mystical search for the Spiritual Father (early tendencies toward
which had occurred in the collection *Early Americana*) and continues
the corollary theme of the assumption of guilt that had appeared in
the non-"westering" short story, "Brothers of No Kin." Like Laban
Oldham, of the story "Early Americana," Brock Brewton experiences
an alienation from his earthly father (or, specifically, his earthly fathers:
Jim Brewton and Brice Chamberlain), a symbol of the Spiritual Father.
His alienation, more pronounced than Laban's, Brock demonstrates not
only by abandoning Jim Brewton's household, but also by altering his
name and turning outlaw. The odyssey of crime, symbolic of Brock's
spiritual quest, culminates in a ritualistic death that somewhat expiates
the sin of his illegitimate birth but precludes a complete reunion with
his earthly (and hence his Spiritual) father. Signifying the partial reconciliation and sounding a final blast at skeptics, Jim Brewton buries
Brock near his ranch house and inscribes, "in unequivocal letters that
all who ride may read," on the boy's headstone: "Brock Brewton, son
of James B. and Lutie C. Brewton."[27] The theme of the assumption
of guilt is exemplified in the actions of Jim Brewton, whose steadfast
ignoring of Brock's illegitimate birth becomes indicative of a desire to
shoulder the sins of his wife. In this respect, Brewton links himself to
Ebenezer Straint, of "Brothers of No Kin," who prayed to be permitted
to assume the guilt of his friend Jeremiah Ritter.

The vastness of these themes to some extent overshadows the characters
in *The Sea of Grass,* and in less skillful hands than Richter's this
tendency would have left the players little better than stock performers
in a melodrama. In certain respects, the characters actually are types—
hero, heroine, villain. But, as Walter Campbell rightly insists, type
characters "are demanded in great historic and poetic tragedy like the
passing of free grass. And very great literature—if it comes to that—
can do very well with type characters; witness the Greek tragedies. The
whole point of *The Sea of Grass* is that the characters are cast away
at the mercy of great forces."[28] In any event, the characters transcend
the types to which they conform, and three of them further assume

importance by functioning as the psychical center of the novel's three divisions: part 1, "The Colonel"; part 2, "Lutie"; and part 3, "Brock."

With the exception of the Reverend Harry Donner in *The Waters of Kronos* and *A Simple Honorable Man,* Colonel Jim Brewton is Richter's finest male characterization. And in several ways, Brewton invites comparison with the minister of the later novels. Although a rancher accustomed to violence, he shares with the minister the same qualities of integrity, courage, vigor, and perseverance. In much the same manner that Harry Donner is dedicated to his ministry, Jim Brewton is devoted to ranching and the land. His loyalty to his own, including his wife, Lutie, and his son Brock, who betray him, is comparable to Donner's fidelity to his parishioners, even those who stray outside the fold. If Brewton does not turn the other cheek in his clash with Brice Chamberlain and the nesters, he, like Harry Donner, still asks no more than his measure.

Brewton's characterization has been criticized for not being very complex, a complaint with some validity. But his lack of introspection in part represents an authorial concession to reality. A frontier rancher's preoccupation was of necessity with external and utilitarian matters more than with philosophical. And in a land ordered more often by the revolver than the court of law, the ambiguity of good and evil never deterred a trigger finger. Moreover, lacking as he is in complexity, Brewton still is more reflective than the stereotyped westerner such as Zane Grey's Lassiter or Owen Wister's Virginian. In fact, Brewton stands somewhere between Walter Van Tilburg Clark's idealistic Arthur Bridges and his pragmatic brother Curt, representing the best of the two extremes. One would have to search long, therefore, to find a more authentic character in western fiction.

Lutie Brewton, the heroine, likewise emerges as one of the most successful creations of a ranch woman that fiction has so far achieved. In the conventional sense, of course, she actually is not a ranch woman, and this deviation from the pattern is the principal reason for her successful characterization. The stereotyped western mother stoically accepts the fate that brings her to a harsh land, and goes silently about the everyday duties of rearing children and maintaining a home, often engaging in work physically demanding enough to transform her (if she survives) into a near-man. Any qualities of beauty and grace she may have had soon become dissipated. But Lutie Brewton, who is vivacious, gracious, and compassionate upon her arrival from Saint Louis, resists hardship. The delicate femininity to which she stubbornly clings is symbolized by the faint odor of violets with which the narrator, Hal Brewton, always associates her. In turn, she symbolizes grace and beauty in a land hostile to both, and her refusal to adjust to hardship is more nearly a commentary on the excessive demands of life than it is on human frailty. Femininity enables Lutie to stand in marked contrast with her husband's rocklike presence. And the result is a complementary impression of fully integrated characterization. Lutie's failure is not from weakness of character (although she does stray into an affair with Brice Chamberlain and subsequently abandons children and home for fifteen years), but from the external conditions of the frontier with which she will not compromise. Because of the theme of sin and guilt with which she is associated, Lutie earns a place beside Hester Prynne, but her position is less substantial because of its lack of passionate justification. Of all Richter's eastern women, Lutie Brewton is superior—longer-lived than Jary Luckett of *The Trees* and less a pawn of fate than Miss Bartram of *The Fields* and *The Town.*

The character Brice Chamberlain is drawn less successfully by Richter, whose villains always emerge short of being fully dimensional. Probably because of the author's kinship to ministers and his rigid subscription to ethical and moral values, the forces of evil in his fiction lack motivation. That Brice Chamberlain could covet Jim Brewton's free range for others (the nesters), therefore, is less understandable than the fact that he could want Brewton's vivacious wife, Lutie, for himself. Even less understandable are the reasons for Chamberlain's remaining in Salt Fork rather than following Lutie into her fifteen years of exile. Despite this lack of motivation, however, Chamberlain's characterization transcends that of the stereotyped villain, for it is shown realistically to be both good and evil, the good reflected in his defense of the nesters. And his characterization is memorable for its contribution to the theme—its role in hastening the demise of the free-range land.

In character, point of view, and plot *The Sea of Grass* has been compared by some critics with Willa Cather's *A Lost Lady.* Among the few dissenting voices raised against Richter's novel, in fact, the common complaint was this similarity. *The Sea of Grass* is "so similar in tone and in theme to Miss Cather's *A Lost Lady,*" said Dorothea Brande Collins, "that not to take cognizance of the similarity would be disingenuous."[29] But, while correctly noting remote parallels between the two works, Collins errs carelessly in referring repeatedly to Richter's Colonel Jim Brewton as "judge"; more crucially, she ignores the point that *The Sea of Grass* blends in such a way into the corpus of Richter's thematic unity as to make it decidedly his own work. For this reason, one may well agree with the estimate that, unless "Miss Cather is to be credited with inventing the heroine who strays," Collins and others misunderstand Richter's novel "by comparing it to *A Lost Lady*."[30]

Actually, Richter's novel *The Lady* bears stronger resemblance to *A Lost Lady;* and other novels by Cather may be invoked to show where Richter succeeds and fails in *The Sea of Grass.* Richter magnificently renders the southwestern landscape, as Cather does in *The Professor's House;* but he fails to transcend it as she does in *Death Comes for the Archbishop.* The quiet ending of *The Sea of Grass,* for example, finds the abortive farms wasteland and points to a later time when even the ranch would die and be "quartered today like a steer on the meatblock." It leaves the principal characters drained and sedentary. By contrast, *Death Comes for the Archbishop* ends on a triumphant note for the principal character, Father Latour. Although he dies, the priest is surrounded by parishioners and others whose fidelity he has slowly won by a life of good works.

More precisely, Richter and Cather resemble one another only in their mutual mourning of the passing of the frontier and the pioneer spirit that, to Richter, is "tamed now, broken and gelded like the wild horse and the frontier settlement." For this reason, the correspondence is no more significant than that between Richter and Elizabeth Madox Roberts, with whom he shared a preference for folk materials; or between Richter and A. B. Guthrie, who also portrays strong pioneer types.

Tacey Cromwell

Having earned his literary spurs as a novelist with the widely acclaimed *The Sea of Grass,* Conrad Richter after 1937 devoted most of his efforts to long fiction. Three of these novels—*Tacey Cromwell* (1942), *The Lady* (1957), and *The Mountain on the Desert* (1955) virtually completed Richter's southwestern writing. Interestingly, the novels of the 1950s were written after the author returned home to Pennsylvania.

Before producing *Tacey Cromwell,* his second novel with a southwestern background, however, Richter had published *The Trees* (1940), the magnificent first volume of his epic eastern historical trilogy. And the fact that he had become immersed in this larger work helps account for the inferiority of *Tacey Cromwell,* which elicited from William DuBois only faint praise for ringing "true in its major premise" but adverse criticism for not stirring "the heart."[31] Likewise moderately praising the novel's successful "local color," a reviewer for the *Nation* attacked its "cinematic" conception and its failure in the "realization of its characters."[32] The *New Republic*'s reviewer argued that "an undertone of repression is present which the author, obviously, has mistaken for restraint."[33]

These rebukes of *Tacey Cromwell* and other of his works created a smoldering resentment that eventually erupted in Richter. In a 1951 letter to the editor of *Current Biography,* the author sought to refute the criticism of his novel, contending that "serious students of the old West" had written him that they understood what he was trying to do—demonstrate that frontier gamblers and prostitutes could be successfully absorbed into respectable community life—and that they believed he had succeeded. Specifically, Richter cited Will Keleher, whom he called "dean of authorities of frontier days in the Southwest" and whom he quoted as having said, "I fiddled around for forty years to write *Tacey Cromwell,* but you beat me to it." Especially did Richter resent the suggestion by *Current Biography* he had written the novel for "the cinema."[34] Shortly after dispatching his letter, Richter, nevertheless, did sell the story to Universal-International, which produced the motion picture.

Richter no doubt conceived of parts of *Tacey Cromwell* as the result of talks with a geologist and his wife who knew the history of the southwestern mining people. In part, he relied on his own experience in mining. From these and other sources he reconstructs the copper mining community of Bisbee in territorial Arizona toward the end of the nineteenth century. To it have come the gambler Gaye Oldaker and his mistress Tacey Cromwell, seeking to rise to respectability and to make a good home for themselves and Gaye's young half-brother, the narrator Nugget. Nugget Oldaker, whose real name is Wickers Covington, had fled from Kansas to avoid harsh treatment by the uncle to whom he had been entrusted after the deaths of his mother and father. Following wagon trains along the Santa Fe trail, the nine-year-old boy had gone first to Socorro, New Mexico, where Gaye and Tacey plied their trades at the White Palace saloon, gambling hall, and house of prostitution.

Thrust into unplanned but welcomed parenthood, Tacey determines to give over her old life and start anew; and she prevails upon Gaye to take the three of them to Bisbee, four hundred miles away. There the family rents a house in brawling "Brewery Gulch," a setting inspired by the "Fighting Hill" mining community for which Conrad Richter's father had served as minister in Pennsylvania during the author's youth. In marked contrast with "Brewery Gulch" stands the "Quality Hill" section of Bisbee. Tacey's family life is decorous and quiet; Gaye has taken employment as a faro banker at the Empire Saloon, and, to the family he supports, Tacey adds Seely Dowden and her baby brother orphaned by a mine explosion. But if Gaye wins respect as an honest gambler, Tacey finds the attempted rise to respectability more difficult. A delegation of women from "Quality Hill," headed by the mine owner's daughter Rudith Watrous, prevails upon the court to remove the children from Tacey's care and to place them in "respectable homes." Tacey remains on the scene as a dressmaker, but is abandoned even by Gaye, who takes a bank position for employment and Rudith Watrous for wife and who eventually becomes territorial treasurer. Nugget becomes a promising mining engineer; but Seely Dowden, whose care had been entrusted to Rudith Watrous, never finds her niche in the respectable world into which she is thrust; she experiences an unfortunate marriage, the loss of a stillborn child, and has several affairs with men. After Gaye's wife Rudith dies suddenly, Seely, Nugget, Tacey, and Gaye experience an improbable reunion.

This event, a flaw of plot, is but one of several crucial weaknesses in *Tacey Cromwell*. Another trouble spot is point of view, which causes fault to arise from merit. Like *The Sea of Grass* a novel of reminiscence, *Tacey Cromwell* is told by a narrator even younger than Hal Brewton during much of the time in which the action occurs. In thus casting Nugget Oldaker as youthful enough to be innocent of the social implications of the story but precocious enough to be shrewdly observant of the results, Richter is able to maintain his authorial preference for muting the lurid and for avoiding moral comment.[35] In other words, this point of view, as Bruce Sutherland suggests,[36] enables Richter to accomplish what Bret Harte could not do with a similar situation. Harte had no choice but to end his *Outcasts of Poker Flat* in tragedy. To have permitted Oakhurst and the Duchess to survive only to return to a life of sin would have flaunted the mores of a provincial society that had developed no scheme for the acceptance of reformed gamblers and prostitutes. But what Harte did not attempt Richter accomplished in that Gaye Oldaker and Tacey Cromwell are a gambler and prostitute who attempt with some success to rise to respectability.

If Richter's point of view enables him to surpass Harte, however, it fails to permit him to transcend the imperfect characterization of Tacey. She suffers from improper motivation as a result of the inability of the narrator to understand the social implications of the story. Gaye might be acceptable as a gambler sincerely wishing to find a less parasitic profession, as John T. Flanagan correctly asserts; but Tacey is harder to accept: "the scarlet woman with the heart of gold whose reform is perhaps genuine but is not made convincing. Her life does not have the passionate justification of sin that makes Hawthorne's Hester Prynne memorable; she is cold and marmoreal."[37] For that matter, neither is Gaye convincing as a character. In failing to make believable the gambler's relationship with Tacey, or even with his half-brother Nugget, Richter forces the character to function merely as a narrative device to further illuminate the woman's altruism and the boy's appreciation of her.

The other two significant characters—Seely Dowden and Rudith Watrous—are stock, the former an example of willful and tragic youth; the latter, of the soft eastern woman unable to adjust to the harsh life of the West. Yet both are interesting because of their affiliations with similar characters in Richter's fiction. Seely belongs in the tradition of Brock Brewton of *The Sea of Grass* and of Rosa Tench of *The Town,* whose youthful tragedies are greater only by virtue of their deaths. Rudith Watrous invites comparison with Amity Bayley, the china-doll character in *The Free Man,* and, by reason of her being the daughter of a mine operator, with Lucy Markle of *Always Young and Fair.*

Set during the early community stage of the processes of "westering," *Tacey Cromwell,* on the conscious and physical planes, promotes the theme and corollaries of human endurance. This concept relates to Richter's theory of evolutionary progress. Tacey endures and prevails against natural and human forces that, in turn, introduce such corollary themes as loneliness, social injustice, freedom versus restraint, the eager heart rejected, and the attempt to rise to respectability. In her loyalty to Gaye and to the children is inherent the theme of altruism. And here, as in the earlier short story "The Laughter of Leen," the altruistic acts are directed toward the living. They are spent on the dying in Richter's first story dealing with the theme of altruism, "How Tuck Went Home."

Like "The Laughter of Leen," *Tacey Cromwell* also advances the theme of brotherhood and human understanding. But, whereas the plea of the shorter work is in behalf of a nation's wartime enemy, that in the novel is for the individual. Tacey Cromwell is a reformed prostitute against whom the "respectable" women of the community rail. And through such shortsighted opposition, the novel illustrates the need for understanding of human frailty. Another difference between the presentation of the theme in the two works is that, while the story belongs to Richter's non-"westering" fiction, the novel derives its theme out of the processes of "westering." Thus, brotherhood and human understanding in *Tacey Cromwell* actually are corollaries of the larger theme of enduring and prevailing.

On the subconscious and mystical levels, *Tacey Cromwell* revolves around the theme of the search for the Spiritual Father. Nugget Oldaker, deprived of mother and father early in life, is alienated from the uncle substituting for his earthly (and hence a symbol of his Spiritual) father. Inherent in his fleeing to his half-brother, Gaye, is a desire for the understanding and love normally afforded by the parent. This desire is symbolized by the light in the western sky to which Nugget is attracted. "I could see through the crabapple tree a luminous light," says the lonely child. "Exactly what there was about that light I cannot say except that it was something against the lonely night to come. Also, it was golden like the house had been when my mother was here, and it lay toward the West where I thought her spirit would like to be, near Gaye in the Territory of New Mexico."[38] This light, as Nugget was to discover through Gaye's unenthusiastic reception of the boy, however, is "false as a gypsy. It might look bright enough back in Kansas. But once you were close, it came through the window gray and mocking."[39] And this realization further alienates the boy from the father-image (now Gaye), both earthly and spiritual.

Such continued alienation results in Richter's adding prominently for the first time a new dimension to his theme of the search for the Spiritual Father: that the mother, whose arms symbolize love, provides a key to the understanding of the father. This variation of his theme Richter had played briefly in the earlier short story "The Old Debt," and he performed it with greater range in *The Lady* and especially in the autobiographical novels *The Waters of Kronos* and *A Simple Honorable Man*. However, in the character Tacey, whose love binds Nugget and Gaye, the author makes his point abundantly clear in this novel.

Finally, as a second mystical theme, the assumption of guilt appears in *Tacey Cromwell*. That Gaye might prosper and the children enjoy the advantages of affluent homes and foster parents, Tacey in effect shoulders the sins of both herself and her gambler-consort. Her selfless act recalls the assumption of Jeremiah Ritter's guilt by Ebenezer Straint in the short story "Brothers of No Kin" and Jim Brewton's acceptance of the sins of his wife, Lutie, and son Brock in *The Sea of Grass*.

The Lady

Fifteen years elapsed between *Tacey Cromwell* and Richter's fourth novel with a southwestern setting, *The Lady* (1957). In the interim, Richter had completed the final two volumes of his monumental historical trilogy, *The Fields* (1946) and the Pulitzer Prize-winning *Town* (1950); and he had published four other novels (*The Free Man* [1943], *Always Young and Fair* [1947], *The Light in the Forest* [1953], and *The Mountain on the Desert* [1955]), and several short stories. By both quantitative and qualititative reckoning, he had become a significant figure on the American literary scene.

The Lady entrenched Richter's position, receiving critical reaction, which, unlike that to *Tacey Cromwell*, proved gratifying to the author. Oliver La Farge, himself the author of the Pulitzer Prize-winning novel *Laughing Boy*, called *The Lady* "enchanting."[40] Similar praise was forthcoming from Coleman Rosenberger[41] and Edward Weeks. "Conrad Richter," said Weeks, "writes with undimmed luster his novels of historic America."[42]

Before it appeared in book form, *The Lady* (like four of its predecessors: *The Sea of Grass, The Free Man, Always Young and Fair,* and *The Light in the Forest*) had appeared serially. Its publication in the *Saturday Evening Post* (30 March and 6, 13, and 20 April 1957) however, marked the final example of such a publishing pattern for Richter. With the exception of isolated episodes, published as magazine short stories, all subsequent novels appeared initially in book form.

The Lady is based in part on actual event. On 31 January 1896, a Colonel Albert Fountain and his young son disappeared between Tularosa and Las Cruces, somewhere in the White Sands country of New Mexico. Their disappearance was the subject of many articles and historical comments. In appropriating this chapter from history, Richter retained the locale and even Colonel Fountain's first name for his character Judge Albert Sessions, but he set his novel several years before the actual event. Still another source were neighbors of the Richters in Albuquerque: a Mexican couple, the wife being the daughter of "a Mazatlan ship building family and a Scotch sea captain." In the novel, the "Lady" is of English and Mexican descent.

Like *The Sea of Grass, The Lady* is a story of violent feuds in New Mexico, but the fighting is between cattle ranchers and sheepmen (not nesters). The rival parties symbolize opportunism and established power, and in the end avarice is defeated by death and the power is dissipated.

The story, again like *The Sea of Grass* and *Tacey Cromwell,* is told by a middle-distance narrator, the motherless boy Jud, who is ten years of age when it opens and about fifteen when it ends. Jud relates the story, however, sixty years after the actual action; whereas Hal Brewton of *The Sea of Grass* tells his only twenty-five years later.

When Jud's father disappears (many think he has run away with a large sum of money entrusted to his care by the commission house for which he is a clerk), the boy is taken into the home of his cousin, United States Territorial Judge Albert Sessions, and the cousin's wife, the "Lady" Ellen. The daughter of a Mexican mother and an English father, Ellen, or Doña Ellen, as she is formally called, is the mistress of a sheep ranch as big as a kingdom. Consistent with her inheritance, she is charming, arrogant, unpredictable—"the child of several races, with long lines of conflicting ancestors rising in her from the past for a moment or two before falling back into the rich and ancient blood stream."[43] If inheritance has given her these physical attributes, as well as land, herds, money, and power, Doña Ellen has provided herself with splendid horsemanship and marksmanship with a rifle. Neither inheritance nor self-provision, however, has given her for a brother-in-law the unscrupulous, mercenary lawyer and villain of the story, Snell Beasley.

Through Doña Ellen's ranch-house grounds and over her protest Beasley's cattlemen drive a herd of steers. The shot that kills one of the drivers is attributed to Doña Ellen's brother Don Carlos (Charley); but, after he is acquitted of the crime, many wonder whether the sister herself had actually pulled the trigger. In any event, the killing of the cattleman looses a chain of violence, which costs Doña Ellen the lives of her brother (slain by cattlemen), her husband, and her eleven-year-old son Willy (both of whom disappear). Bereft of the men who might have defended her, Doña Ellen faces the loss of her ranch to Snell Beasley.

At this juncture, one of nature's creatures comes to the rescue. An expert driver of fast horses, Doña Ellen has been known in part for her trotter Critter, which refuses to be passed by any other horse. In younger days Critter had no challenger, but now in his older days he is confronted by a horse Snell Beasley has purchased expressly to make Doña Ellen's defeat at his hands complete. The race between animals and drivers results in an accident fatal to Beasley, and it provides Critter and his mistress with the final triumph.

In addition to the similarity of titles, parallels of characterization and of technique make Richter's *Lady* somewhat analogous to Willa Cather's *Lost Lady*.[44] Each work features as the protagonist a woman of social position, grace, intelligence, and arrogance. Between Richter's Doña Ellen and Cather's Marian Forrester, however, are sharp differences. Doña Ellen is wealthy in her own right and has the ability and determination to oppose hardship. When she loses possessions and husband, rather than sinking to the level of a paramour or of an opportunist, she resolutely faces adversity and triumphs over it. Never does she become "a lost lady," and, for this reason, she transcends the narrow definition given early in the novel by one of the characters, who says a lady is "a woman of great charm or position who because of it has never had to do anything for herself but has always had someone to do for her."[45]

But even if Doña Ellen is a fully developed character, her story leaves unanswered a troubling question: was it she, an expert marksman, whose shot killed the cattleman and triggered the violence? The question recurs at intervals, and rises up, as the end approaches, when Ellen says, "I hoped it could be done without further bloodshed, but now I see he [Beasley] must be dealt with as the dog he is."[46] And, while events move toward this climax, the narrator Jud broods over the "contest between good and evil, or was it between evil and evil?"[47] After the final violence, when one might expect a weighing of the scales, Jud appears to have forgotten this somber question.

Similarly, a question arises in *A Lost Lady* in which the final status of Marian Forrester is merely implied by her having left the country. But the failure of both Cather and Richter to be explicit does not affect the finality of their stories: the narratives of Marian Forrester and Doña Ellen are complete.

Technically, *The Lady* and *A Lost Lady* resemble each other in brevity and in point of view. Richter, as in his other two southwestern novels, reveals his story through a young man, who is related to one of the principal characters and who maintains close but detached interest in the action. Willa Cather likewise employs as narrator a young man, even less linked to Marian Forrester than Jud is to Doña Ellen, who nevertheless frequents the Forrester house. Because of their youth and relative insignificance, both narrators leave many gaps in their stories, which proceed by widely separated episodes and by suggestion rather than by continuity and detailed reporting. For Richter, at least, this technique allows him to place less emphasis on violence than on the loneliness of a desert graveyard and the vastness of the aloof and silent land. From such a distance, his story becomes not melodrama but a tale of far-off things, "the most haunting of earlier happenings in the annals of New Mexico."[48] Jud, however, is the last narrator that Richter uses in his fiction.

Set during the ranching stage of the processes of "westering," *The Lady* presents themes growing out of this march of civilization. Doña Ellen's adoption of the young narrator Jud, for example, illustrates altruism, a corollary of the theme of enduring and prevailing, which, in turn, is representative of Richter's theory of evolutionary progress. In this respect the novel resembles the earlier *Tacey Cromwell,* in which a similar adoption occurs. Both of these instances, like that in the early "Laughter of Leen," find the altruistic acts directed toward the living. Such acts are spent on the dying in Richter's first story built around the theme of altruism, "How Tuck Went Home."

In revealing the close bond between Doña Ellen and her horse Critter—between a human being and one of nature's creatures—Richter explores for the final time in his fiction the organic unity of humans and nature. This theme recalls his theory that all life is governed by natural laws. Richter had first promoted the concept in his earliest stories, *Brothers of No Kin,* and he continued to do so in *Early Americana, The Sea of Grass,* the historical trilogy, and *The Light in the Forest.* Most of these works illustrate the theme by bringing people into contact with the land; but some—such as "Smokehouse," "The Man Who Loved a Hound," and "Long Drouth," like *The Lady*—do it by depicting the relationship between people and nature's creatures. In any event, the result on a subconscious and mystical level almost invariably is the glorification of nature, contributing either to the corollary theme of the idyll of the farm (the old agrarian myth) or the mystique of the wilderness. The latter theme is developed in part in *The Lady* through evocative description such as that in a reverie by the narrator Jud. Riding with his cousin Willy, Jud remarks that they "were prisoners suddenly escaped to the unfettered world of land and sky." The scene, he says, "was the older, more joyous world where the Creator and the Mark of His hand were still to be seen and felt." Experiencing such a scene, Jud adds, "gave us a feeling of the largesse of God and of receiving favors directly from His hand."[49]

Finally, on the subconscious and mystical levels in *The Lady,* the theme of the search for the Spiritual Father parallels that in *Tacey*

Cromwell. Both examples focus attention on the mother, whose arms symbolize love, as the key to the earthly (and hence the Spiritual) father from whom, in this case, Jud feels an alienation. Jud's own father disappears, presumably having run away with stolen money but actually having been murdered by robbers. And Doña Ellen, in taking the boy into her own home, becomes in effect his mother. In this connection, Richter, in a letter, said: "In *The Lady* I tried to get a look at the lady symbol of America, of the early tendency of both America and the symbol to use arms and their final turning to tolerance and love for the solution of their quarrels."[50]

Having come reluctantly to the Southwest, Conrad Richter accepted his "fate" that was New Mexico and profited mightily by it. While restoring the health of his wife, the region inspired the author to turn to the type of fiction he would do best—historical. The collected stories *Early Americana,* the novels *The Sea of Grass, Tacey Cromwell, The Mountain on the Desert,* and *The Lady* earned Richter a secure place both in southwestern and in national letters.

Richter's southwestern novels, it is true, are smaller in compass and design than his eastern historical novels. And while there is in the eastern novels a strong, natural flow of life, one finds in the southwestern novels problem stories, more complicated and less reflective. Yet, as Walter Havighurst correctly claims, Richter's southwestern fiction is "always lyrical, evoking the moods of the land and the commitments of its people."[51]

In a sense, Richter's southwestern fiction belongs to the curious nationalism of the depression, when writers as divergent as Van Wyck Brooks and Kenneth Roberts sought to find in the past answers to problems of the present. This literary rediscovery of America, insists Dayton Kohler, will be recorded as a remarkable phenomena of a confused age. Suddenly, in a period ostensibly dominated by economic determinism and social reportage, the sense of the past, carrying the impact of a new idea, demanded articulation. As critics have remarked, this compulsion to reclaim the past amounted to an invocation.[52]

But many of the writers turning to the past overlooked the patterns of continuity with the present and focused instead on antiquarianism, uncritical and often sentimental. "My complaint over some of the tremendous tomes which have been produced by modern novelists," says T. M. Pearce, is that few of the heroes or heroines have been worth the amount of reader time they have consumed. The authors have worked hard to provide reader interest (and have frequently succeeded) but the art of arousing interest and the art of re-creating a way of life in a past forgotten day are not the same thing. Few of these modern literary behemoths of history and romance have yielded the end product I demand in fiction, which is to bring me the philosophy of an age, the moral and ethical pattern in the period, the motivation and incentives for people to live as they did.[53]

Writing with simple human warmth and vigor, Richter vividly portrayed character and event without being bound by history per se. In this wise he has accurately captured "the philosophy of an age, the moral and ethical pattern in the period, the motivation and incentives for people to live as they did." Historical fiction can make no greater demand of the literary artist.

Chapter Five

The Pennsylvania–Ohio Trilogy

Significantly, Conrad Richter followed his eminently successful first novel, *The Sea of Grass,* a stirring history of his adopted Southwest, with *The Trees* (1940), the first volume of an epic historical trilogy of his native Pennsylvania-Ohio region. The publication of *The Trees* revealed the author's versatility in capturing the essence of history in two diametrically opposed geographical and cultural areas, and it further showed him to have retained the memory of native ground from which he had been absent twelve years. As a result of this achievement, as well as that of the earlier *The Sea of Grass,* the Society of Libraries of New York University in 1942 conferred upon Richter its gold medal for literature. And the award on the basis of his first two novels demonstrated that Richter, unlike many writers, had successfully avoided a traditional pitfall of following a brilliant initial work with an inferior second one.

While still a resident of the Southwest, Richter completed the eastern trilogy, with the publication of *The Fields* (1946) and *The Town* (1950). Between *The Trees* and *The Fields,* however, he inserted *Tacey Cromwell* (1942), his second southwestern novel, and *The Free Man* (1943), a history of Colonial Pennsylvania. And between *The Fields* and *The Town,* he worked on *Always Young and Fair* (1947), a period piece set during the late nineteenth and early twentieth centuries in Pennsylvania.

The Trees

For both content and style *The Trees* received immediate critical acclaim. "Richter makes skilful use of his evidently profound historical studies," wrote Rosamond Lehman, "and the picture of pioneer life he builds up is extraordinarily concentrated, detailed and vivid."[1] Praising the novel's fidelity to historical change, Richard Cordell said, "Like the sound of the axe in the final curtain of 'The Cherry Orchard,' the crashing of the great hickories at the end of *The Trees* signifies the passing of an era."[2] Rose Feld and Max Gissen, respectively, acclaimed Richter's prose as "holding the accents of poetry"[3] and as being "spare, lyric."[4]

The Book-of-the-Month Club purchased rights to the novel in March 1940 and thus prepared the way for its becoming Richter's best-selling work. But when Twentieth-Century-Fox Studios attempted to buy the movie rights, Richter refused for reasons he explained more than twenty years later in a letter to the motion picture producer Tom Gries, who also wanted to buy the movie rights to *The Trees*. When the novel was first published, Richter said Fox had offered him twenty-five thousand dollars for the film rights. "A short time before this," continued the author, he had been "very deep in debt" and even at the time of the offer "the money would still have been very welcome." Because *The Trees* was the first volume of a projected trilogy that Richter was still uncertain he could complete, however, and because Richter believed that Hollywood could not realistically produce quality historical works— for both reasons, he said, he declined the Fox offer. Later, he declined still other offers.[5] But in 1979, eleven years after Richter's death, the National Broadcasting Company filmed all three volumes of the trilogy and televised them in a splendid mini-series, *The Awakening Land,* starring Hal Holbrook and Elizabeth Montgomery as Portius and Sayward Luckett Wheeler.

Set in the Northwest Territory west of the Alleghenies and north of the Ohio river in the late eighteenth and early nineteenth centuries, *The Trees* is told omnisciently in carefully constructed episodes. The episodes here, as well as in *The Fields* and *The Town,* are closely related in that the character Sayward is the psychic center of each. In *The Trees* unfolds the common story of the typical pioneer family: its migration from Pennsylvania through the endless forest, its building of a cabin, and its trials and tribulations in clearing the land.

Worth Luckett, the "woodsy" father and born hunter, had been west as a boy with Colonel Boquet, whose expedition to reclaim white captives of the Indians informs Richter's novels *The Light in the Forest* (1953) and, inferentially, *A Country of Strangers* (1966). Now, with game retreating in the face of civilization in western Pennsylvania, Worth takes his family—his sickly wife, Jary; his daughters Sayward, Genny, Achsa, and Sulie; and his son Wyitt (a sixth child is left in an infant grave)—into the wilderness. Near a spot covered with deer antlers, the sign of a plentiful supply of game, he builds a cabin.

The darkness under the big trees and the debilitating effects of fever depress the mother, Jary, who soon dies at the age of thirty-seven, leaving the responsibility of rearing the younger children largely on the sturdy shoulders of fifteen-year-old Sayward. Sayward's self-sufficiency is illustrated in part by her drowning of a buck deer that provides the table meat her father has neglected to bring home.

Other settlers drift into the area, and one of them seeks Sayward for his wife. She declines the proposal, however, privately asserting that, though he might be the first prospective husband around, he probably would not be the last. But if Sayward refuses to marry, her sister Genny does not. Genny becomes the bride of Louie Scurrah, a "woodsy" who as a child had acted as a decoy for Delaware Indians on the warpath and whom Sayward intensely dislikes. Sayward's suspicion proves prophetic, for Louie eventually abandons Genny and runs off with her sister Achsa to the English lakes.

Meanwhile, a trading post is set up on the river by George Roebuck, one of whose patrons, the brutal Jake Tench, skins a wolf alive and then sets the animal free. Such examples of "civilization," coupled with the disappearance of his baby daughter Sulie, provoke Worth Luckett to abandon his other children and to push farther into the wilderness, ostensibly in search of Sulie whom he thinks has been taken by Indians. Sayward thus is left with permanent responsibility for young Wyitt, himself destined to become a vagabond hunter like his father, and for Genny, who has returned to the family cabin after being abandoned by Louie Scurrah. No further word of Sulie nor Worth is heard for years by the family.

When Jake Tench decides that Portius Wheeler, the Bay State lawyer going to seed in the wilderness, needs a wife, Sayward agrees to take him for her mate. The wedding, however, is performed while Portius is drunk; and, when the startled bridegroom discovers what has happened, he flees. Brought back by Jake Tench, Portius remains with Sayward, whom he treats with gentle deference and even assists in cutting down trees for a garden patch. Happily Sayward looks forward to her firstborn.

That *The Trees* and the other volumes of the trilogy had been conceived as an artistic whole, there can be no doubt. Richter's purpose from the beginning, he wrote to Edward Weeks, "was to start with an early American woods character who knows only a rude hunter's cabin, and to take her, together with the great region in which she lives, from wilderness to cultivated fields to town."[6] And, indeed, such purpose had been evident in Richter's short story "Rawhide Knot"

(*Saturday Evening Post,* 1 January 1938), which anticipates much of the entire trilogy.

In the short story, the principal character, Sayward Hewett, is the model for the protagonist, Sayward Luckett Wheeler, of the novels. Like the later heroine, she marries a Portius Wheeler (whose name remains the same in the trilogy). Also unchanged are the names of such characters as Jake Tench and George Roebuck. Sayward Hewett's sisters, as in the novels, are named Achsa, Genny, and Sulie; but her father, Thomas, becomes Worth Luckett and her brother Michael becomes Wyitt in the novels. Also changed is the name of Granny Wildermuth (of the story) to Granny MacWhirter. Finally, a change of relationship occurs with Beriah, who is a granddaughter of Sayward in the story but an aunt in *The Trees.*

"Rawhide Knot" also provides the answer to an unsolved riddle in the trilogy. In the novels, the reason is never clear as to why Portius Wheeler, an educated lawyer from Boston, has come to the wilderness. Sayward thinks it has been because of his rejection by a woman he loved, but this is only conjecture. In the story, when Sayward agrees to marry the drunken Portius, she is told by Jake Tench: "They was a high-toned Boston woman he wanted to marry once. He don't want the likes of you."[7]

On one level in *The Trees,* Richter promotes (for the first time in his fiction set other than in the Southwest) the themes growing out of the processes of "westering." He does so without resorting to the glamor of historical pageantry—without, that is, carefully staged dramatic situations, great names, or great deeds. "The natural simplicity of the story," as Bruce Sutherland says, "is in itself a work of art."[8] The characters are common people portrayed in the daily and yearly rounds of their primitive existence: their heroism is enduring and prevailing. Richter's preference for writing about such persons and for writing about them in their own idiom, he said, derived in part from the inspiration of Caroline Miller's *Lamb in His Bosom.*[9] In part, his preference derived from the "remnants of American pioneer stock" he had known in his youth and in remote Clarks Valley and New Mexico slightly later in his life.

Through these common people generally and the protagonist Sayward specifically, then, Richter demonstrates in *The Trees* his themes growing out of the processes of "westering." The theme of restless wandering, for example, is illustrated by Worth Luckett, who flees with his family from what he considers to be the constrictions of civilization and who, when even the Ohio frontier becomes too peopled to suit his tastes, abandons family and pushes even farther west. In the process initially, Worth is mildly opposed by his wife, Jary, whose protest illustrates a second theme: the hunter's drive in conflict with the settler's instinct. Both this idea and that of restless wandering represent Richter's theory of "inharmony." Jary's loss of the struggle in premature death makes her an example of a character Richter employs to illustrate the theme of the inability of eastern woman to adjust to primitive western conditions. In this sense, Jary is similar to Lutie Brewton of *The Sea of Grass* and to Miss Bartram of *The Fields* and *The Town* who, although spared life, are equally unable to adjust. This theme is a negative corollary of the concept of enduring and prevailing; and it reveals realistically that, in the course of "westering," people do not always succeed. The theme of enduring and prevailing, in turn, recalls Richter's philosophical theory of evolutionary progress.

It is mainly Sayward, the principal character, who represents two of the major themes growing out of the processes of "westering" on the physical level. In assuming at the early age of fifteen a mother's responsibility for her younger brother and sisters, in providing for the family after the desertion of their father, and in countless other ways indicative of her self-reliance, strength of body and character, and perseverance, she illustrates the theme of enduring and prevailing as well as the concept of evolutionary progress. And her triumph over primitive conditions by the novel's end suggests the passing of the frontier or the theme of historical change.

Worth's "woodsy" ways exemplify the theme of the organic unity of humans and nature, an idea linked with Richter's theory that all life and matter are governed by natural laws. But Jake Tench, who brutally skins a wolf alive and then releases the creature to run suffering through the woods, is suggestive of the ambivalence of the relationship.

All of these themes obtain mainly on the level of physical action. On the psychological level evolves what Frederic I. Carpenter has called "a kind of symbolic tale of the American unconscious, in which the mythical pioneer reverts to savagery, both in action and thought, in order to deal with the savagery of the wilderness." This level of myth and symbol suggests "the dark night of the soul which accompanied the racial experience of Americans, almost unique in the history of civilization, and the gradual 'illumination' which followed."[10]

This theme of the traverse of the American racial unconscious from "the dark night of the soul" to "illumination" had been anticipated in *The Sea of Grass* and earlier in *Early Americana*. Both works evoke images of a landlocked sea—the title itself in the novel and the references, in "Smoke over the Prairie," to a "gray, imprisoning sea"; and, in "The Square Piano," to "the vast grassy sea of our Rafter P range." In *The Trees*, which changes the locale from the Southwest to the East and the time from the late nineteenth to the late eighteenth century, the sea of grass becomes a sea of trees: The Lucketts "moved along in the bobbing, springy gait of a family that followed the woods as some families follow the sea," writes Richter in the novel's opening sentence.[11] From the top of the Alleghenies, the family catches its first glimpse of the West, of "a sea of solid treetops broken only by some gash where deep beneath the foliage an unknown stream made its way."[12]

From this point, however, the Lucketts plunge down beneath the sea of treetops to enter a strange "dark country" submerged under "that ocean of leaves."[13] They enter a dark, green subsurface—"sometimes subconscious and sometimes almost subhuman"[14]—world of primeval, uncivilized wilderness. "A man's mind," says Richter, "had stranger and darker ways than a beast in the woods. You could poultice a body wound or a snakebite and it would draw the poison out. But try and do that to a woodsy's mind and you only drove it in."[15] Such a wilderness produces a wildness of the mind like that of the brutal Jake Tench or like "some red beast out of one of Sulie's nightmares."[16] Even the gentle Genny, gifted of voice in song, who, abandoned in her isolated cabin when Louie Scurrah ran off with her sister Achsa, could approach her brother Wyitt and peer "at him as if half blind from living in a dark world."[17]

If these events symbolize the "dark night of the American soul," the conclusion of the novel represents the beginning of "illumination." After bringing Genny back to the family cabin, Sayward remarks that never "had it felt so good at last to see a cloud of white shining ahead through the dark trees."[18] And, when Portius Wheeler has been rescued from his wilderness ordeal by his marriage to Sayward, it seemed as though Sayward "stood high above the trees where she could look out over a vasty sea of leaves."[19]

This theme is further reinforced by ritualistic scenes. First is the preparation for and burial of Jary, whose feet are placed toward the East and the rising sun. Another occurs at the end of chapter seven, "Maidenhead," when Sayward, having removed her clothing and plunged

into the river to bathe, suddenly becomes aware that she is now a
woman and thus rejoices:

Then for a while she stood to dry, inspecting with matter-of-fact criticalness
her strong breasts and hams.
Yes, she was a woman now, she told herself, a white woman in this
country of the men of the Western waters. It was good enough being a
woman. She didn't know as she'd change it now, had she the chance.[20]

In chapter 17, "The Ever Hunter," Wyitt's initiation as a hunter is
portrayed; and in the final chapter, "Black Land," Sayward and Portius's
battle with and triumph over the trees in clearing a patch for their
garden ritualistically signals the beginning of a new way of life.[21]

The Fields

Between *The Trees* and *The Fields* (1946), second volume of his
Pennsylvania-Ohio historical trilogy, Conrad Richter interlaced a second
southwestern novel, *Tacey Cromwell* (1942); a historical novel of colonial
Pennsylvania, *The Free Man* (1943); and several short stories. During
this period World War II had drawn the United States into its net,
causing novelists and others to divert at least part of their effort to
patriotic and even propagandistic activities. *The Free Man,* although set
during the American Revolution, reflects the pitfalls of purposive writing.
But whatever its shortcoming, Richter compensated for it by writing
The Fields and the short stories.

The stories, interestingly, consisted often of episodes that Richter
would employ in *The Fields.* "The Face at the Winder" (*Atlantic,* May
1945) forecasts the strange prophecy about and death of Sayward
Luckett Wheeler's infant daughter Sulie, whose namesake—Sayward's
sister—likewise had experienced tragedy in *The Trees.* And "The Nettle
Patch" (*Atlantic,* January 1946) predicts the encounter that one of
Sayward's sons would have with a rattlesnake in *The Fields.*

The Fields was met with mixed critical reaction. Theodore M. Purdy
praised the authentic details, "the phrases of the dialogue, the hymns
sung at the prayer meeting," but he complained that "one might admire
Mr. Richter for his exactitude on those points and still not count him
a good novelist."[22] Most other reviewers, however, were more favorably
impressed. "How difficult it is to evoke real life like this," said Alfred
Butterfield. "Writers who can treat of good and evil without sitting in

judgment; who have sureness of step among the intricacies of human emotions; who have a knowledge of and sympathy for their characters transcending either experience or research—such writers are few. Conrad Richter is one of them."[23]

Outwardly very little happens in *The Fields* because large scenes are not needed to show what the novel purports to do: to demonstrate the hard work and slow growth that built the frontier community. The setting, as in *The Trees,* is the Northwest Territory in what is now southeastern Ohio, but the time has shifted from the late eighteenth to the early nineteenth century. Actually, the year 1803 is the only exact date in the novel, which covers about two decades.

When Sayward and Portius Wheeler's first child, a son named Resolve, is born, the father is away at the Chillicothe convention that had ratified the constitution making Ohio a state. And upon his return, he refuses at first to look at his son. Sayward tells herself that Portius should get accustomed to children because she intends to fill the cabin with them. Then, making her intention good, she promptly adds three more to the household: a second son, Guerdon, named for her close-mouthed uncle "back along the Conestoga"; a third son, Kinzie; and her first daughter, Sulie, named for her sister who had been lost as a child in the forest. Her first son, Resolve, Sayward had had christened by the circuit rider in the crude sawmill church at which Sayward's sister Genny loves to sing but to which Portius, a disbeliever, refuses to go.

By the time the Wheelers' fourth child had been born, their community had been designated a township, and on Old Christmas the first taxing list had been made out during a party at Sayward's cabin. When the list is completed, the people realize that civilization has become an accomplished fact.

Before Sayward's first daughter, Sulie, had been born, Resolve thought he had seen a strange little black boy, dressed in white, peeking in the window. The apparition becomes prophetic, when, at the age of three, Sulie dies of burns received in a fire. Resolve, seeing her charred body, pulls at Sayward's skirts to indicate to his mother that the body lying in the coffin is really not his sister but the black boy he had seen peek in the window.

Following the mass slaughter of night dogs preying on farmers' livestock, Sayward's brother Wyitt realizes that the game has departed the nearby woods. Without saying goodbye to his sister, who he fears would keep him on the farm, he heads west as his father Worth Luckett had before him.

By now Sayward has given birth to two more daughters, Huldah and Libby, increasing to five the number of her living children. To educate his growing brood, Portius starts a school and teaches in it himself until his law practice in Tateville grows so large that he is compelled to bring in a woman instructor, a Miss Bartram. Having had two more daughters, Sooth and Dezia, Sayward decides that seven living children are enough and withdraws from marital relations with Portius. Her withdrawal leads to an affair between Portius and Miss Bartram, whose illegitimate daughter Rosa, as Sayward notes, fills the gap between Sayward's Dezia and her daughter Mercy, born out of the reunion of Sayward and Portius. Before giving birth to Rosa, however, Miss Bartram had married Portius's crony Jake Tench.

Continuing to employ the omniscient point of view and the tightly designed episodic structure (with Sayward as the psychic center), Richter relates the story of *The Fields* in the same homely idiom of its predecessor *The Trees*. Here, however, the effect is somewhat strained. Rather than employing the idiom naturally, the author now encloses in quotation marks such expressions as "yaller" for yellow and "cam" for calm. His purpose perhaps is to indicate the changing times: to show Sayward, to whom the expressions are attributed, to be something of an anachronism in an area rapidly becoming civilized. If so, the technique performs its function, but it also contributes to the impression that the idiom is artificial.

Again through the characters generally and Sayward particularly, Richter employs themes growing out of the processes of "westering." But because the time is that of the community, rather than of the frontier, stage of "westering," he focuses on ideas related to this phase of the alteration of the wilderness to farmlands and to the beginnings of a community. In other words, he dwells on the theme of historical change. And with such change, as civilization encroaches on the wilderness and farm, the problem of freedom versus restraint occurs. Such a theme is exemplified in Wyitt Luckett's decision to flee westward, a decision that also illustrates the theme of restless wandering especially pronounced in *The Trees*. Historical change is related to Richter's theory of evolutionary progress, while restless wandering bears on the concept of "inharmony."

Civilization also tends to relegate to a subordinate position the theme of the organic unity of humans and nature, an idea suggestive of Richter's philosophical theory that all life is governed by natural laws. For this reason and also because nature is ambivalent, *The Fields* presents a negative corollary—the life and death of the land—through a drought that ruins the farm crops.

Through Sayward, who, having survived the ordeal of the wilderness trek and having successfully reared eight of nine children, the theme of enduring and prevailing is demonstrated. The deaths of her little daughter Sulie and of her neighbor Jude MacWhirter (the victim of rabies) illustrate, however, negative corollaries: the tragedy of youthful death and of the hostility of nature. The illicit relationship between Portius Wheeler and Miss Bartram suggests still another negative corollary of enduring and prevailing: the eager heart rejected, a theme that appears also in *Tacey Cromwell* and in *The Sea of Grass.*

On the level of symbol and myth, *The Fields* continues what Carpenter terms the theme of the making of the American racial unconscious. In *The Trees,* this theme had suggested the traverse from the "dark night of the soul to illumination," as the pioneers gradually emerged from beneath the sea of trees into the sunlight. In the marriage of Sayward and Portius—she practical and wise although unlettered, and he lettered, but often impractical and unwise—is implied "the strange mixture of pioneer realism with puritan idealism which has gone into the making of America."[24]

Portius's infidelity to Sayward provokes the wife to seek solace in a manner recalling Richter's theory of human energy supply and expenditure. In his philosophical essays and novel, Richter had advanced the theory that the human organism, when hungering for energy to meet a challenge (in this case, Portius's infidelity), could acquire the necessary energy through activity. Here, Sayward hitches her oxen to the plow and works all day in the fields. That night she feels healed of her heartache.

Overall, Sayward is representative of the Great Mother. As such, in *The Town,* she would become related to the mystical theme of the search for the Spiritual Father, a quest to be undertaken by her last child, Chancey. As shown earlier, the mother (whose arms symbolize love and understanding) functions as a key to the earthly father (himself a symbol of the Spiritual). The minister's wife in the earlier short story, "The Old Debt," and Tacey Cromwell and Doña Ellen Sessions of *Tacey Cromwell* and *The Lady,* respectively, perform similar functions.

A second mystical theme in *The Fields* is the assumption by one person of the guilt of another. Sayward's sympathy for the plight of Miss Bartram, mother of an illegitimate child by Portius Wheeler, is indicative of her symbolic assumption of Portius's guilt. The theme of the assumption of guilt had also appeared in the short story "Brothers of No Kin" and in the novel *The Sea of Grass*.

The Town

Before publishing the final volume of his Pennsylvania-Ohio historical trilogy, *The Town* (1950), Conrad Richter made his first and only excursion into tragicomedy with *Always Young and Fair* (1947), the tale of a twisted romance during the Spanish-American War and its aftermath in a Pennsylvania town almost identical to Pine Grove. He also published several stories, one of which anticipated his National Book Award-winning novel, *The Waters of Kronos* (1960).

On the basis of critical acceptance, *The Town* stands as Richter's crowning achievement not only in the trilogy but in the entire body of his works. It received the Pulitzer Prize in 1951, and it drew admiring praise from several fellow novelists. Louis Bromfield applauded Richter's work as "distinguished and poetic both as to character and image." Richter, he added, "has the supreme gift of novelists in creating a world of utter reality in which the reader is able to lose himself completely after the first page or two."[25] Walter Van Tilburg Clark praised "the integrity of Mr. Richter's performance."[26]

To an extent, of course, the Pulitzer Prize represented belated recognition of the earlier volumes of the trilogy and especially of the first, *The Trees*. And undoubtedly *The Town* falls short of *The Trees* in evoking atmosphere. But, as T. M. Pearce rightly insists, *The Town* "brings to the reader the gist of Conrad Richter's meaning in writing the other books,"[27] and for this reason it tends to offset its limitations.

Set in the pre–Civil War period in Ohio, *The Town* completes the story of Sayward Luckett Wheeler, who has seen the wilderness give way to farmlands and to community and who here finishes the course of her life. Sayward's death in her eighties does not come, however, until after she has given birth (in her late forties) to her tenth and last child, the frail Chancey; seen her eldest son, Resolve, marry into wealth and become governor of Ohio; witnessed a daughter become the wife of a titled Englishman; suffered through the unfortunate marriage of her son Guerdon to a slut, whose lover he kills and then flees, leaving his sprightly and prophetic little daughter Guerda to become the favorite of her grandmother, Sayward, before dying (after telling Sayward she had dreamed a good angel was coming for her) of a throat infection; moved unwillingly into the new brick house Portius deems necessary to a family of such stature as his (Sayward has become the wealthiest person in town) and to the furniture he has inherited from his Aunt Unity in the Bay State; welcomed back her father, Worth, returned from nomadic wanderings in the West; accompanied her sister Genny to an unsuccessful interview with an Indian squaw, who they think is their sister Sulie, the one who, in *The Trees,* had disappeared as a child in the woods; and survived Portius in death.

Although she shares the stage with her youngest child, Chancey, Sayward Luckett Wheeler continues in *The Town* to be the central figure she is in *The Trees* and *The Fields.* The story is told in her idiom, but not in the first person. And it continues to promote her pioneer virtues. She possesses the self-reliance, perseverance, and fortitude essential not only to survival but to crowning success. And while basically undemonstrative, she is intensely loyal to her own—even to her errant husband Portius and to her rebellious son Chancey. These are qualities, anticipated as early as the short stories "The Laughter of Leen" and "Wings of a Swallow," that come to flower here. In many respects, they recall the qualities imbued in Colonel Jim Brewton of *The Sea of Grass.* In *The Town,* as throughout the trilogy, of course, Sayward "is only superficially like the simple pioneer women whose statue stands in hundreds of American town squares from Ohio to Oregon—or like the Lucinda Matlock of Spoon River who 'at ninety-six had lived enough, that is all, / And passed to a sweet repose.' "[28] She is more complex, combining virtue with occasional cruelty, willfulness, unenlightenment, and domination. Indeed, she is one of the truly memorable women in American fiction.

Sayward's husband, Portius Wheeler, however, is the most unusual character in *The Town* (and in the entire trilogy, for that matter). And he illustrates a problem of characterization that continued to trouble Richter. On the one hand, Portius is the embodiment of virtue. He is educated, shrewd, humorous (in a dry fashion), and passionately sympathetic with the underdog. So long as he is portrayed in any or all of these ways acceptable to the author personally, he is successful as a character. But, on the other hand, Portius is agnostic, unfaithful, and given to drink. And he often fails, when shown in these guises, to be a credible character because of the lack of proper motivation he shares with all the errants or the villains in Richter's fiction. Richter simply never understood deviant behavior.

In completing the life story of Sayward and Portius, *The Town* also brings to full cycle the processes of "westering" begun with pioneer settlement in *The Trees* and continued with agricultural and early community development in *The Fields*. In this Pennsylvania-Ohio trilogy, Richter accomplishes therefore the supreme undertaking of honestly portraying the essence of American experience. With restrained realism instead of romantic excesses, he depicts pioneers with their hopes, trials, and achievements. Several artistic devices other than characterization enable the author to perform his task.

One such device is the generous use of authentic folk materials gleaned from oral sources. In a letter to John T. Flanagan, Richter said that he considered the Lucketts to be a mixture of Scotch-Irish and Pennsylvania Dutch "either in blood or environment." The colloquial speech he attributes to his characters, he added, derived not from any literary source but from listening to the language of his family and early friends in small Pennsylvania towns: "My good luck was that I heard most of it spoken and learned unconsciously when and how it was used."[29]

From such sources, then, Richter derived northern dialectal terms such as "Diel" for Devil and such expressions as "I don't give a hait for it." He resurrected archaic words such as "plunder" for possessions, "snake doctors" for dragonflies, and "night dogs" for wolves. And he appropriated standard illiteracies, homely idioms, chapter epigrams ("Spit on your hands and take a fresh holt"), proverbial sayings ("Come day, go day, God send Sunday"), apothegms ("The tree casts its shade upon all, even upon the woodcutter"), superstitions, medical lore, and old ballads. Closely related to the use of folk materials as a device for accomplishing his purpose in the trilogy is Richter's simplicity of style. Here, as in all his fiction, it is characterized by understatement. Only in the plotted complexity of *The Town* does Richter deviate from simplicity, and he does so merely to indicate that life itself has become complex with the advent of civilization. Finally, humor enables Richter to accomplish his purpose and to serve as a reminder to the reader that pioneer life was not always grim. Under the author's treatment, humor varies from the practical jokes of Jake Tench to the sophisticated wit of Portius Wheeler, who swore witnesses and even several judges on a "Bible" that actually was a well-worn copy of *Arabian Nights*.

In completing the processes of "westering," *The Town* emphasizes the theme of historical change that grows out of the march of civilization from wilderness to farm to community. Such change, in turn, connects to Richter's theory of evolutionary progress. In this novel, it is illustrated overall in the realization of full community status for Sayward's residence, which had started as a crude cabin in the forest. It is demonstrated on the level of individual characters in the relationship of Sayward and her youngest child, Chancey. Sayward, who represents the pioneer's views, and Chancey, who is the epitome of modern social thinking, are in conflict not unlike that represented by a similar dichotomy in Hawthorne's *House of the Seven Gables.* At first employing direct and old-fashioned methods, Sayward tries to make a pioneer-type man out of her son, to whom she is unable to communicate the values of an earlier generation. But, when Chancey leaves home to edit a liberal newspaper that attacks his brother Resolve (the governor, who is quite like his mother), Sayward secretly supports the struggling newspaper. Not until near the end of the story, when he learns of his mother's patronage, does Chancey begin to achieve understanding: "Was there something deeper and more mysterious in his mother's philosophy than he and his generation who knew so much had suspected; something not simple but complex: something which held not only that hardship built happiness but which somehow implied that hate built love; and evil, goodness?"[30] But his discovery is too late. His futile cry "Mama!" indicates not only that Sayward has died but that from this time forward Chancey "would have to ponder his own questions and travel his way alone."[31] He had shut his eyes to the older generation and had thus deprived himself of values essential to life.[32] At this point, Chancey assumes a resemblance to young John Gant of Richter's short story "Smoke over the Prairie." Upon regaining consciousness following the wreck that killed his father, Frank Gant, the boy searches the crowd for the missing man and cries, "Where'd he go?" It is a cry that Richter himself raises for a past generation whose values he considers fundamental.

Further illuminating the point that Richter is making about historical change, in an earlier scene Sayward's father, Worth Luckett (returned from his odyssey in the West), confronts Portius Wheeler's "Bluestocking" sister from Boston:

"Americus must be very grateful to you, Mr. Luckett," she [the sister] pronounced.

"What fer?" Worth asked suspiciously, looking at her direct for almost the first time.

"Judge Wheeler just told us. For founding such a growing city in a new land."

"I had no idee o' that," Worth told her tartly. "Or I'd never settled here. . . . Town scum . . . stick in one place. They go through the whole rumpus of gettin' born and dyin' and have no idee how the Lord Almighty meant them to live."[33]

Conrad Richter's complaint is with some facets of historical change that accompany "westering"—change that simultaneously destroys and builds, as civilization subdues the past and leaves strewn in its wake those who resist it. Here, as in all of his historical fiction, Richter is confronted with the same duality that bothered Cooper: civilization is at once good and evil.

It is as though Richter were saying (in both his eastern and southwestern historical works) that formerly a virgin land rolled under carpets of grass resembling a sea up to the slopes of mountains, tree-dotted with pine and spruce, then naked save for patches of snow crowning the summits. Winds rippled the grass, rustled the leaves, and howled above the timberline. But the chill, except at the higher altitudes, abdicated to the sun that bathed the land. Here roamed the Indians, unobtrusive residents of antiquity, taking only what was necessary for sustenance—and that insufficient to despoil the grandeur of the setting. Later even the Spaniards, who would have despoiled everything in their mad quest for Cibola, retreated in the face of space and time. In their wake they left descendant the passive Mexicans, who were enough Indian to take little more than they needed. Not until the whites did the land surrender its maidenhead to "progress," suffer itself to be ravaged by the plow and the gleaming rails of the iron horse that drained the sea of grass, uprooted and subjected the native Indians and dominated the docile Mexicans until their want in truth became the far side of Cibola. The ravishment, however, took six centuries in the American Southwest.

Two thousand miles away in Pennsylvania and Ohio, civilization wedged its way with surer, faster strides. Not Spaniards seeking gold, but the English and German and Scotch-Irish in search of land—soil to be cleared of trees and plowed and tilled; earth on which to raise cabin, town, and city—brushed aside the Indian tenants and failed to absorb them into the bloodstream of family lineage. Here, the rape of the land and banishment of the Indians took less than two centuries.

Whether late in coming, as in the Southwest, or early, as in the East, civilization still performed at least one selfless office by creating a pioneer spirit. Pristine qualities of bravery, hardihood, stoicism, and frequently even decency the white settlers developed or plumbed from untapped reservoirs within themselves. And having found the new resources, some of them even resented the civilization for which they had prepared the way. And rightly should these few resentfuls have objected to their handmaiden. Civilization now has come to Pennsylvania and Ohio and, although less certainly with a pall of mushroom cloud, to the Southwest. In its wake it has left not stubborn Yanks to ring a liberty bell in defiance of oppression nor even tranquil Mexicans to blend into a natural way of life. Its effect, at least to Conrad Richter, has been that the "lusty pioneer blood is tamed now, broken and gelded like the wild horse and the frontier settlement" (*The Sea of Grass*).

Or, as Richter expressed the detrimental effects of historical change in an essay, the modern people have lost those early American qualities of "hardihood and vigor"; of "manliness," not "physique," but "a quality of mind and spirit," still more "of creed and belief." Moderns have failed to retain from their forebears "a sense of sovereignty, a rank vitality, and a deep unswerving belief in the dignity of man, beginning with" themselves. They have neglected to retain "oratorical enlargement," the "hearty and profound vigor of thought and phrase," and "continence."[34]

In marshaling such apparently conflicting combinations as the urban Chancey Wheeler, on the one hand, and his "woodsy" grandfather, Worth Luckett, on the other, *The Town* presents a mystical corollary of the theme of the organic unity of humans and nature. Organic unity is representative of Richter's theory that all life is governed by natural laws. In *The Town,* it takes the proportions of a mystique of the wilderness, a theme evident in Chancey and Rosa Tench's love for nature and in old Worth's hostility toward civilization that despoils nature.

Also on the mystical and subconscious level, *The Town* brings to fruition the theme of what Carpenter calls the making of the American racial unconscious. It does so through the relationships of Jake Tench and his wife and of Chancey Wheeler and Rosa Tench, the latter Mrs. Tench's (or Miss Bartram's) daughter by Portius Wheeler. Reminiscent of Huck Finn's father, Jake Tench is in marked contrast to his romantic wife. The name "Tench" derives from a fresh-water fish, allied to the dace and id, noted for its tenacity of life, and Jake Tench embodies the subhuman and merely instinctive in American life. On the other hand, his wife, who neurotically shuts herself off from society after their marriage, embodies the romantic, bookish, and antirealistic in American life. Allowing her household to deteriorate and her children to grow up without parental direction, she reads borrowed novels in her dirty chimney corner. And in such an environment Rosa Tench grows up.

Like Hawthorne's Pearl, Rosa is the natural child of sin and romantic idealism; and, like Hudson's Rima, she loved the woods but is also familiar with the sordid sides of the town. Never having been told the truth of her birth, she yet feels that Jake Tench is not truly her father. "And when her lover, Chancey, ignobly deserts her for reasons she cannot understand, she commits suicide by disemboweling herself with an eel-spear, as if trying to exorcise the animal element of her human nature."[35]

In depicting the incestuous love of Chancey and Rosa, Richter follows Melville before him in American literature and Robinson Jeffers contemporary with him. Richter's treatment of the mythological theme, however, is more realistic than Melville's and less sordid than Jeffers's. It is what Carpenter calls "a new combination of realism and restraint."[36] Richter achieves such balance by juxtaposing the idyllic, as when Chancey and Rosa wander off from the public picnic into the seclusion of the deep woods by the river—the idyllic, that is, with the realistic, as when Chancey forces back to earth the hot-air balloon that Rosa had freed by cutting the anchor rope. The descent of the balloon symbolizes the fate of their "stealthy union of earth and heaven," which ends tragically.

Embittered by the fate that has provoked his and Rosa's tragedy, Chancey experiences an alienation from his and Rosa's earthly father Portius Wheeler. And his attempt to find consolation illustrates Richter's theme of the mystical search for and reconciliation with the Spiritual Father for whom the earthly father is a symbol. First, Chancey visits his mother's Protestant minister, but "nothing rose to the good doctor's lips save piety and justice and the uncompromising word of God."[37] Then, after unsuccessfully visiting the Catholic priest of the Tenches, the boy turns to his earthly father. But "his father sat there noble and untouched."[38] Chancey derives a brief moment of consolation from the fanatic "Old Johnny" Appleseed, who babbles mysticism out of Swedenborg's *Heaven and Hell;* but at the end Chancey is left by Richter to continue the quest alone. Like Brock Brewton of *The Sea of Grass,* True Son of *The Light in the Forest,* and Stone Girl of *A Country of Strangers,* he is unable to effect an understanding of and a reconciliation with the Spiritual Father.

Chancey's problem is compounded by his failure to understand his own mother. Under Richter's treatment of the theme of the search for the Spiritual Father, the mother becomes a key to an understanding of the earthly (and hence the Spiritual) father. Such is the case in "The Old Debt," *Tacey Cromwell, The Lady,* and *The Waters of Kronos.* In failing to understand Sayward, then, Chancey deprives himself of a rather certain avenue to an understanding of the Spiritual Father.

In character, authentic detail, style, and theme, the Pennsylvania-Ohio trilogy of Conrad Richter ranks beside *The Time of Man* by Elizabeth Madox Roberts. Indeed, in scope, it transcends Roberts's work. So effectively has Richter reproduced the life of the pioneer that, long after any vestige of our forebears remains, one may read *The Trees, The Fields,* and *The Town* and know precisely what it was like in an era when (within two or three generations) a frontier wilderness became transformed into a teeming civilization. Such a reader will discern, too, that the material and spiritual values of the earlier age—perhaps not enough of which have been salvaged—are applicable to any time: that what we are is the product of what we were, and that what we will become depends upon our learning the lessons of earlier generations. Even thus informed, however, contemporaries, like the pioneer, will find that the course is never easy—"death and birth, grub and harvest, rain and clearing, winter and summer." But they, just as their earlier counterpart, must take one with the other. For, to Richter, "that's the way it ran,"[39] and that is the way it will continue to run.

Chapter Six
Interludes

From the time he began writing novels, Conrad Richter intentionally or otherwise interlaced with his major projects less ambitious ones. In all, eight of these minor works that resemble interludes were published. The first, *Tacey Cromwell* (1942), Richter's second southwestern novel, appeared between the first two volumes of Richter's celebrated Pennsylvania-Ohio historical trilogy, *The Trees* (1940) and *The Fields* (1946). Likewise appearing in the same period was Richter's unimpressive *The Free Man* (1943). A third interlude, *Always Young and Fair* (1947), was published between the second and third volumes of the historical trilogy, *The Fields* and *The Town* (1950). Following *The Town* but anterior to Richter's impressive southwestern novel *The Lady* (1957), appeared his fourth interlude, *The Light in the Forest* (1953). Finally, between the first two volumes of a projected autobiographical trilogy (the accomplished *Waters of Kronos* [1960] and the equally gifted *Simple Honorable Man* [1962], with the third volume uncompleted at Richter's death in 1968), the fifth through eighth interludes appeared: *The Grandfathers* (1964), *A Country of Strangers* (1966), *Over the Blue Mountain* (1967), and *The Aristocrat* (1968). These eight interludes almost seem to be respites from the creative rigors of the more ambitious works being undertaken by Richter. Yet they were by no means—nor were they intended to be—light exercises to keep authorial techniques sharpened for bigger things. For that reason and others, then, the impression that the eight works represent breathing spells results more nearly from artistic lapses than from intention.

The Free Man

The second of eight interludes, *The Free Man*, ran serially in the *Saturday Evening Post* (15, 22, and 29 May and 5 June 1943) before it appeared in book form. In this respect it parallels *The Sea of Grass*, which preceded it, and *Always Young and Fair*, *The Light in the Forest*, and *The Lady*, which followed it. Of all Richter's novels, *The Free*

Man received possibly the sharpest critical rebuke. Conceding that the story starts "extremely well," Ben Jones complained that it ends as "a Hollywood costume piece."[1] Even Edward Weeks, one of Richter's staunchest admirers, protested that "for the first time in his career" Richter "has been inhibited by the limitation of the short novel."[2]

A major reason for the novel's shortcoming is its purpose to inspire the present with lessons of the past, for Richter was writing in the midst of World War II. "Perhaps in an understanding of the Pennsylvania Dutch, their loyalty to democracy and their love of peace," wrote Richter in the preface to the novel, "may be found the secret of a peaceful Europe in the years to come." Such purposive tendencies, of course, were not new. American literary figures as early as Philip Freneau, of the Revolutionary War era, had similarly weakened their art in behalf of a cause. And when Richter turned to the same Revolutionary War for examples to inspire his own age, he likewise faltered.

It must be conceded, however, that *The Free Man* was timely in recalling the occasionally neglected fact that American freedom sprang from European roots. Set mainly in Walnut Mills, Pennsylvania, near Reading and Harris's Ferry, from shortly before to well after the American Revolution, the story is told as reminiscence. The principal character, who relates the tale to his nephew and a lawyer Hartranft (also a writer for the Reading newspaper), is Henry Free. Born Henry Dellicker, he is a prosperous storekeeper and former soldier and Congressman, a character modeled after Conrad Richter's maternal great-great-great-grandfather, Henry Conrad, and his son Frederick. As an eighteen-year-old boy, Henry Free had sailed with his parents and four hundred other Swiss and Palatines from Rotterdam to Pennsylvania. Short on rations and plagued by illness, Henry's mother and father (as well as many others) die aboard ship. Under the pretext that, blown off course, he will have to land at the dreaded Martha's Vineyard rather than at Philadelphia, the ship's captain succeeds in tricking the surviving passengers to sign additional papers of indentured servitude. Under such an arrangement, Henry Free is bound for five years to an Englishman named Richard Bayley. The master's young cousin, Amity Wigmore Bayley, renames the servant John in order to avoid confusion with her uncle and brother, both named Henry. Smarting from this and other indignities heaped upon him by the spirited Amity, Henry runs away. After being temporarily captured at Reading, he escapes to a frontier trading post; there he becomes successful and wins the respect of the pioneers with whom he conducts business. When the Revolutionary

War breaks out, Henry recruits sixty men and prepares to join the fight. En route to battle, he is once again arrested on orders from Amity. She tells Henry that her late father had purchased his indentureship from her cousin and that now he is beholden to her. The difficulty is resolved, however, when Henry and Amity marry. He goes off to battle and is wounded. But recovered and returned home, he launches a successful career in business and politics.

Evident in this synopsis is one of the novel's basic weaknesses: the improbable union of the lowly Henry Free and the aristocratic Amity Bayley. Although mutual revolutionary war enthusiasm could conceivably have brought these two opposite personalities together, the difference in social station should have kept them apart. More understandable would have been a match between an English woman and a German man from the same social strata.

Moreover, this flaw of plot underscores a more crucial failing of characterization. *The Free Man* is a vignette; as such it should provide a much clearer picture certainly of the protagonist, Henry Free, and also of his antagonist-turned-mate, Amity Bayley. In the effort to impress upon the reader Henry Free's love of freedom and his difficulty in earning it, however, Richter stresses brutality at the expense of affection, which is necessary to bind the reader to the boy. This, as Edward Weeks correctly concludes, is "a problem of selection, and it is still more besetting in the second half, where there are too many gaps in Henry's life for us to see him whole or to know him with familiarity. How did he really tame his Shrew? What were they like as man and wife? And why did they have no children? These are the questions we really want to see answered, and without them the story must seem cold and secretive."[3] Moreover, the failure of Richter to depict Amity Bayley as a rounded personality results in her emerging as something more nearly resembling a china doll than a flesh-and-blood person. It links her with a character likewise inadequately portrayed, Rudith Watrous of *Tacey Cromwell*.

Despite their flaws of characterization and their improbable mating, Henry Free and Amity Bayley in marriage do perform the service of illustrating one of the themes of the novel. Through the union of German and English, Richter, echoing Crèvecoeur, presents the theme of America as a melting pot of ethnic groups. It is a concept that the author had dealt with previously in "As It Was in the Beginning" and with which he would deal again in *The Light in the Forest, The Lady,* and *A Country of Strangers*. The melting-pot concept is a corollary of the larger theme of historical change, which, in Richter's fiction, grows out of the processes of "westering." And *The Free Man*—set earlier than any other of the author's works growing out of such processes—thus demonstrates that, virtually from the beginning of European civilization in America, ethnic lines dissolved through marriage. In turn, the themes of change and America as a melting pot recall Richter's philosophical theory of evolutionary progress.

Henry Free's successful fight for freedom represents a second theme related to "westering": hardship-into-gain. The hardship—the adversity—harks back to Richter's theory of human energy supply and expenditure. In his philosophical works, the author insists that adversity enables an individual to draw on supplies of energy from his or her own organism and consequently to satisfy an energy hunger. In *The Free Man* he implies that people are collectively enabled to satisfy the hunger for freedom by undergoing adversity. The theme of hardship-into-gain here is a link in the chain that extends throughout Richter's fiction.

The scope of Henry Free's life further stands for the theme of enduring and prevailing, a concept closely related to Richter's philosophical theory of evolutionary progress. But, as noted, people do not always endure. The Swiss and German settlers who die aboard the ship that brings Henry Free to America, for example, illustrate the failure. Of these, the youths who die reinforce the novel's theme of the tragedy of youthful death. This theme, a negative corollary, is likewise employed by Richter in *Early Americana, The Sea of Grass, The Lady, The Trees, The Fields,* and *The Town.*

Shoring up these themes, with their overtones of freedom, are at least two obvious symbols in *The Free Man.* The iron collar Henry Free wears as an indentured servant represents forces that restrict human freedom. Queen Street, on which Amity Bayley resides in Reading, stands for aristocracy that would compel others to servitude.

As a historical service, *The Free Man* reveals important but unfamiliar aspects of American nationhood and the part played by the Pennsylvania Dutch with their "little Declaration of Independence" as early as April and May 1775 and with their introduction and development of the pioneer rifle. These actual events, as well as the other themes, result in the novel's making a plea for international understanding and brotherhood. Richter had sounded a similar plea in the short stories "The Laughter of Leen" (1916) and "The Good Neighbors" (1943). And while the first is applicable to World War I, the second, like *The*

Free Man, extends to World War II. Richter's later novels *The Light in the Forest* (1953) and *A Country of Strangers* (1966) carried the theme of understanding and brotherhood, which the author's philosophical works contend to be the essence of evolutionary progress, over to the post–Korean and pre–Vietnamese war periods.

Always Young and Fair

More than twenty years separate two of Richter's interludes, which nevertheless resemble one another in a number of important ways. The first such interlude, *Always Young and Fair* (1947), was produced between the second and third volumes of the author's Pennsylvania-Ohio trilogy, *The Fields* (1946) and *The Town* (1950). Its companion interlude, *The Aristocrat* (1968), Richter's final novel, is interlaced between the second volume of an intended autobiographical trilogy, *A Simple Honorable Man* (1962), and the uncompleted third volume.

Always Young and Fair had appeared in condensed form in the 12 October 1946 issue of the *Saturday Evening Post* before it did in book form. It thus paralleled publishing patterns of the earlier *The Sea of Grass* (1937) and of the later *The Light in the Forest* (1953) and *The Lady* (1957).

For setting and characters in *Always Young and Fair,* Richter turns for the first time since his short stories of 1913–33 to the Pennsylvania of his youth. Pine Mills is the actual Pine Grove, and many of the characters are modeled after persons either related to or well-known by the author. The novel is dedicated to Augusta R. Filbert of Pine Grove, Richter's cousin by marriage, whose house and that of her Uncle Dan serve as background for the story. Miss Filbert is the Georgia of *A Simple Honorable Man* (1962), which builds on several scenes in *Always Young and Fair.*

The return to familiar scenes for fictional materials prompted Richter to indulge in nostalgia to the extent that critics complained. Cassie Meredith, for example, insisted that the "period novel should not rely too heavily on nostalgia, accuracy of detail, and exact observation. Characters must be vital enough to inspire some reaction. In the case of *Always Young and Fair,* the cast, without any exception, have no real being."[4] Complaining similarly about nostalgic strains, the *New Republic* also assailed the denouement, contending, "Richter owes Faulkner's 'A Rose for Emily' a considerable debt . . . which gives his hitherto quietly nostalgic story a macabre denouement."[5] The denouement, repeated Rose Feld, strains "one's belief."[6] In praising the characterization of Lucy Markle and the faithful portrayal of place, Edward Weeks protested that the novel lacks "the fine edge of temper which makes *The Sea of Grass* vigorous beyond its brevity."[7]

Always Young and Fair begins with the Spanish-American War and extends to the mid-1920s. In essence, it is the story of a representative segment of Teddy Roosevelt's America, of the serene, bucolic life often referred to as the "age of innocence." Its final chapters, however, link the novel with Woodrow Wilson's America. And one of the strong points of the work is its successful re-creation of the spirit of the times and place.

Against that background, Richter again employs a youthful narrator to tell the story of Lucy Markle. Johnny, whose name recalls that of Richter's narrator in the short story "Smoke over the Prairie" and of a major character in the novels *The Waters of Kronos* and *A Simple Honorable Man,* is a third cousin and affectionate admirer of Lucy. Yet, like all of Richter's fictional predecessors, he is sufficiently detached to present an objective account. A portion of his detachment may be attributed here, as in nearly all of Richter's works employing a narrator, to the fact that Johnny for several years is away at college and thus unable to observe directly the events of a given moment.

As related by Johnny, Lucy Markle's story (like that of Jay Gatsby) involves an attempt to stop the clock. In 1898, Private Tom Grail, aged twenty, dies in the service of Company G of the Pennsylvania National Guard in the Philippines. Supposedly he had been engaged to Lucy Markle, then aged eighteen, who, although thought by most actually to love Tom's cousin Captain Will Grail, was felt to be motivated by pity for Tom in her choice between the two.

Upon Tom's death, Lucy busies herself by caring for the dead youth's rheumatic father and in numerous other ways reflecting homage to Tom's memory. Initially, she spurns the marriage offer of Will Grail, and, later, when she has consented, fails to appear for her wedding. The years speed by. Meanwhile, Johnny completes college and becomes an engineer in Lucy's mine (an occupation followed by the narrator Nugget Oldaker in *Tacey Cromwell*); Lucy's mother and father die; and Will Grail serves as a colonel in World War I, returning home physically broken from the recurrence of a tropical ailment acquired twenty years earlier in the Philippines. Will is now forty-five; Lucy, about forty. And whereas he once was solicitous of her every whim, he now ignores her. At a Legion hall dedication, Lucy hears a public reference to herself as a "well-preserved, gray-haired lady." Only then does she realize, in terror and with sudden resentment, that she, like all mortal flesh, has grown old and that only the memory of Tom Grail, to which she has devoted her life, has stayed forever fresh and unchanging—"always young and fair." In feverishly casting herself upon Will Grail, therefore, she prepares the way for the macabre denouement: shortly after their marriage, Will becomes an invalid for whom Lucy must care until the end of his days.

In *Always Young and Fair,* then, Richter has inadvertently veered into tragicomedy in reverse. Traditionally, tragicomedy, of course, is a play with a plot suitable to tragedy but which ends happily like a comedy. Although doubtlessly intended as a serious vignette, *Always Young and Fair* revolves around personal actions so eccentric as to become ludicrous until the denouement, which takes a turn toward the tragic.

The character of Lucy Markle, with her vanity, her growing eccentricities, and her consuming egotism, is clearly drawn. But other aspects of characterization remain faulty. Primary among these flaws is the relationship of Lucy and Will Grail, both of whom live unaccountably long within their own rigid reserve. That Will could be patient at first with Lucy's perversity is understandable; that he does not openly rebel earlier in a more vigorous way is not. Lucy and Will, nevertheless, become the only characters in Richter's fiction to end in tragedy because of their own willfulness, and they thus command greater attention than they might otherwise deserve.

From the characterizations of Lucy Markle and Will Grail emerge the three dominant themes of the novel. The theme of altruism, for example, is inherent in the good deeds that Lucy performs for the dying father of her late fiancé, Tom Grail, and for others. It is a concept that relates to Richter's philosophical theory of evolutionary progress. The theme of altruism is dominant in Richter's first short story "How Tuck Went Home." It also appears in *Tacey Cromwell* and "Good Neighbors." In *Tacey Cromwell,* altruism is a corollary of the theme of enduring and prevailing that grows out of the processes of "westering," but in these other works "westering" is not a factor. One of the minor themes of *Always Young and Fair* that also emerges from the characterization of Lucy Markle, who tries to stop the clock, is the theme of time; this concept becomes dominant in "Doctor Hanray's Second Chance" (1950) and in *The Waters of Kronos* (1960).

In his repeated rejections by Lucy, Will Grail also represents the reverse twist (the masculine example) of the theme of eager heart rejected. Such a theme appears (with feminine examples) in *Tacey Cromwell, The Fields,* and *The Town.* But in *Always Young and Fair,* unlike in the other three works, it does not grow out of the processes of "westering."

Supporting these themes are obvious symbols. The name (Tom) Grail suggests a sort of holy grail for Lucy, whose romantic illusions are symbolized further by the sentimental song:

> Only to see you, darling!
> Only to hear your voice!
> Even the faintest whisper
> Would make my heart rejoice.[8]

Symbolic of the change in Lucy, suddenly realizing that time has passed her by and flinging herself upon Will Grail, is the Oliver story in which a spinster similarly pursues a man.

Perhaps the redeeming feature of *Always Young and Fair* is its anticipation of *The Waters of Kronos* and *A Simple Honorable Man,* the distinguished first two volumes of Richter's projected autobiographical trilogy. The postoffice scene here, for example, carries over almost intact to *The Waters of Kronos,* which also alludes to Markle's colliery (Lucy's father's mine). Also, the narrator Johnny (whose last name is never given) strongly resembles John Donner of the later novels. Finally, the tramp Tom Widener, with whom Lucy is friendly, is the counterpart of Mike Whalen in *A Simple Honorable Man.*

The Aristocrat

Even though written two decades later, *The Aristocrat* (1968) serves as a companion interlude to *Always Young and Fair,* sharing backgrounds and characters. It is Richter's final published novel. Shortly after its publication, the author died, leaving unfinished the third volume of his projected autobiographical trilogy. The first two novels of the uncompleted trilogy, *The Waters of Kronos* and *A Simple Honorable Man,* and *Always Young and Fair* combine with *The Aristocrat* into a kind of personal reminiscence of the kind hearts and genteel people Richter had known while growing up in Pine Grove. As reminiscence can be, *The Aristocrat* becomes the most self-indulgent of Richter's four novels.

The aristocrat of the novel is Alexandria Morley, refined but spirited spinster daughter of a southern-bred mother and a northern father who made a fortune coal mining in Unionville (the fictional Pine Grove). She is a cousin of Lucy Markle, daughter of Alexandria's aunt on her mother's side and the eccentric protagonist of *Always Young and Fair*. Of the two cousins, Alexandria is more stable than Lucy but nonetheless anachronistic, tenaciously clinging to old southern manners in a modern world. She is indomitable in her eighties and provides the voice for Richter's final protest against mediocrity and modernity, which he sees as weaknesses when compared to the accomplishments and principles of earlier generations.

Indeed, Alexandria Morley, resembling what one reviewer called a "Main Street Auntie Mame,"[9] assails a variety of persons she deems guilty of violating her (and sometimes society's) codes of churchmanship, decorum, and honesty. She wins a good many of her battles, such as civilizing young Dr. Clay Howell, competent in the practice of medicine but lacking in manners and general refinement; forcing a large coal company to pay delinquent taxes; preventing a minister from praying aloud over her deathbed; and generally getting her way in a world usually deferential to her.

Some of her battles, however, Alexandria Morley loses. She submits grudgingly to Cousin Eulalie's petitions that she be baptized before she dies, thereby committing an act she had not realized would automatically confer upon her the church membership she had steadfastly refused in the past. She refrains from interfering in her great-niece Hope Connor's difficult decision in choosing one of three suitors for her husband, even though the choice is not one Alexandria would have made. Finally, she helplessly watches the construction of an apartment complex that despoils the landscape, including one of Alexandria's favorite views.

Between her victories and defeats, Alexandria's fights-to-draws engage her attention. One is with the city council over noxious odors from the public trash dump. Other draws are with her cousins, one garrulous and the other envious. Alexandria tolerates both out of her stubborn conviction that family obligations override personal preference.

The events in Alexandria Morley's story are neither numerous nor, finally, very arresting. They require only 135 pages for the episodic telling. Then, following the basic narrative are two curious devices that defy classification. One consists of thirty-nine pages of what Richter calls "Addenda" and presents Alexandria's (and Richter's) pronouncements on her father, maids, relatives, friends, modern times, herself, and other things. The second end-device consists of three pages of what Richter calls a "Cast of Characters Living and Dead" and enumerates Alexandria's relatives and others relevant to the family. Such end-devices represent a critical weakness of the novel, because they treat through exposition matters that should have been presented dramatically in the main narrative. Not since the infancy of the American novel in the early nineteenth century had such devices been used.

If the structure of *The Aristocrat* proves unsatisfactory, however, the point of view is acceptable. Alexandria Morley's story is told by a youthful narrator Tommy Gault, the great-grandson of Alexandria's uncle Jim Morley. Tommy's role, however, results not from his remote kinship, but from his being the son of the man Alexandria calls her "major domo," Martin Gault. Martin takes care of those things around Alexandria's large Victorian house that her women servants cannot do, runs many of her errands, and provides innumerable other services. His primary occupation, nevertheless, is serving as deputy sheriff, a job Alexandria has secured for him.

To place Tommy in a position to be the narrator, Richter assigns to Alexandria the need for a "man in the house" at night, when the regular servants are away. The device is plausible enough, and Tommy proves adequate to the requisites of narrator. Despite his youth, he is a believably astute observer; and, despite his obvious affection for Alexandria, he is detached enough to be fair in dealing even with her adversaries. The use of a youthful narrator affiliates *The Aristocrat* with *The Sea of Grass* and *Tacey Cromwell,* as well as with some of Richter's short stories.

The portrait of Alexandria Morley painted by the youthful narrator leaves mixed impressions because of the materials Richter gives the boy to work with. On the one hand, the protagonist appeals very much to the reader. She subscribes to many of the best ideals of the past and tries mightily to preserve them. At the same time, she is no prude: she smokes and drinks, in moderation, and has a fine sense of humor, as when on her death bed she confounds the condescending minister attempting to pray over her by pretending to confuse him for the bartender at the country club. Patrick Dennis's original Auntie Mame could hardly have done it better than this "Main Street" one.

On the other hand, however, Alexandria is quite obviously anachronistic. Had she prevailed to the ultimate, she would have stopped time and returned life to the past of her youth. She may be quite correct that the apartment complex she resents despoils the landscape, including her favorite view, and that the public trash dump emits noxious odors. Her opposition to them, however, offers no meaningful alternatives.

The main flaw of Alexandria Morley's characterization, though, is that in developing it Richter inadvertently veers into caricature reminiscent of southern romance. After Alexandria tells the reader she was brought up to be polite even if it killed her, the reader expects next to catch: "Fiddle-de-dee, Cap'n Butler, just you mind yo-ah manners."

Additionally, Richter juxtaposes with Alexandria stock characters who might have peopled his less accomplished magazine short stories in his early years as a writer: the brash but bright young doctor, the attractive niece, faithful servants, officious clergymen and politicians, and well-intentioned but inept foils (in this case, Alexandria's cousins) to further illuminate the superiority of the protagonist. Each suffers as a result of Richter's refusal to surrender even a small part of the stage Alexandria dominates. Their insignificance tends to make the novel a sort of dramatic monologue.

Obviously, most of the themes of the novel grow out of Alexandria Morley's characterization. Enduring and prevailing is perhaps the main theme. In Richter's philosophical theories, it frequently is linked with historical change for the better. Here, however, the reverse is true. Alexandria resents much of the change and resists it until her death. Unlike Sayward Luckett Wheeler, who prepares the way for civilization to replace the wilderness, Alexandria merely erects a few roadblocks temporarily halting the pace of change but finally is powerless to stop it. She makes no effort to influence the direction of change. In that wise, her actions point to another theme, the inevitability of change.

Despite its numerous flaws, The Aristocrat is by no means the worst of Richter's interludes. Without resorting to the Gothic devices found in Always Young and Fair, Richter depicts an eccentric old woman with considerable virtue. The reader can empathize with her much more readily than with Lucy Markle. Then, the activities in which Alexandria participates, even while sometimes lacking substance, are certainly more significant than those in the folkloric works The Grandfathers (1964) and Over the Blue Mountain (1967), the latter more nearly a children's book.

The Light in the Forest

Still another of Conrad Richter's interludes, The Light in the Forest (1953) followed the final volume in the historical trilogy, The Town

(1950), and preceded Richter's final southwestern novel, *The Lady* (1957). (Also appearing in this interim was Richter's philosophical novel *The Mountain on the Desert* [1955], but it belongs with the two book-length essays rather than the interludes.) *The Light in the Forest* appeared serially in the *Saturday Evening Post* (28 March and 4, 11, and 18 April 1953) before it did in book form. It thus corresponds in publishing pattern to *The Sea of Grass, The Free Man, Always Young and Fair,* and *The Lady.* Walt Disney filmed it for motion pictures and then television.[10]

Superior to several of Richter's other interludes, *The Light in the Forest* received substantial critical recognition. Lewis Gannett praised the work as an "evocative parable."[11] The *Nation* called it a "touching idyl."[12] And Edward Weeks, although critical of the "moralizing at each end," concluded that the novel "does succeed in probing closer" than he could remember "to the resentment which the Indians felt against the whites and to that inflammable mob spirit which the conquering American too often let loose."[13]

As an objective and realistic historical novel dealing with the relationship between the Scotch-Irish settlers of western Pennsylvania and the Tuscarawa (Delaware) Indians during 1764–65, *The Light in the Forest* has likewise drawn praise from Maurice D. Schamier and others for its fidelity to ethnohistory.[14] In this connection, one might recall that at least three types of historical fiction exist: (1) the period novel, such as Adolph Bandelier's *Delight Makers,* which is written in the spirit of historical research or antiquarianism; (2) the historical romance, such as almost any of Kenneth Roberts's novels, a type designed largely as escapism; and (3) the historical novel proper that does not evade reality. Conrad Richter's historical fiction belongs to both the first and third categories. Richter himself abhors the second. His aim, he said of *The Light in the Forest,* was "not to write historical novels" per se, but "to give an authentic sensation of life in early America."

At least two real-life characters, Colonel Henry Boquet and the Reverend John Elder, appear in *The Light in the Forest.* The presence of Colonel Boquet serves as a reminder that the character Worth Luckett, of Richter's historical trilogy, had been a member of one of Boquet's western expeditions. Among the purely imaginary figures in the novel, Del Hardy (reminiscent of Cooper's Leatherstocking) suggests that Richter, like Cooper, acknowledged the use of John Heckewelder's *Account of the History, Manners, and Customs of the Indian Nations Who Once Inhabited Pennsylvania and the Neighboring States* for much of his background material. An additional source could well have been an actual incident in the early days of Richter's native Pine Grove, where, as the author well knew, the first settlers suffered harassment by Indians:

A well authenticated tradition establishes the family of a Mr. Everhard, consisting of four persons, on the site of Pine Grove, as early as 1755. During the Indian foray of the year last written, the entire family was massacred, except one daughter, aged about seven years. She was taken as a prisoner into the Muskingum country in Ohio, where she lived as a member of an Indian family until the year 1763, when, the Indians being defeated by General Boquet, the white prisoners were liberated under the terms of the treaty. Miss Everhard was recognized by some of the old neighbors, and subsequently married a Mr. Sallada, of Berks county, and became the progenitress of a numerous and prominent posterity. Some of her descendants reside in Schuylkill county, while many are residents of Berks county, and the west. This tradition is verified by a complete record of the events here recorded, carefully preserved in an old family Bible.[15]

Finally, incidents at Clarks Valley, where Richter and his family lived on a farm in the 1920s, likely provided background for *The Light in the Forest*. At the Peter Allen house in Clarks Valley in the late 1600s, as Richter notes in an article, bounties were paid for Indian scalps.

Employing such sources, Richter sets his story in 1765 in the Tuscarawa village at the forks of the Muskingum in Ohio and in western Pennsylvania. Then, using an omniscient point of view and the idiom of both the Indian and the pioneer settler, he relates the experiences of young John Cameron Butler: his captivity and rearing by Indians who name him True Son, his compulsory return by Colonel Boquet to his white parents, his inability to readjust to the white man's ways, and his unsuccessful attempt to return to his Indian foster parents.

As the story opens, John Butler, aged fifteen, has for eleven years been True Son, the adopted son of the Indian Chief Cuyloga, whose own son died from the "yellow vomit." True Son had been captured during an Indian raid on his father's farm in western Pennsylvania and had been taken by his captors to their village on the Muskingum River in Ohio. Having long since adapted to Indian life, he resists the order of the Boquet expedition from Fort Pitt that all white captives be returned to their original homes. Other captives, including the wife of Little Crane, likewise protest, thus surprising the soldiers who have come to rescue them. But the order sticks, and True Son is entrusted to the woodsman Del Hardy in order that he will not escape. For much of the return trek, Half Arrow walks beside his adopted cousin True Son, but at Fort Pitt he is turned back by the soldiers.

Taken to Paxton Township (his birthplace) and returned to his actual father and mother (Harry and Myra Butler), True Son (or John as he is now called) resists attempts to civilize him. At a family reunion, he clashes with his uncle Wilse Owens, who had joined the "Paxton Boys" in a massacre of Indian women and children. One night Half Arrow secretly visits John and takes him to the body of Little Crane, slain by whites while attempting to visit his white wife. Half Arrow and John confront Uncle Wilse with the murder and wound him before fleeing to the Indian village. Reunited with his Indian parents, John joins Cuyloga and his braves in avenging the death of Little Crane. When John sees Thitpan massacre white children, however, he experiences a moment of truth: the Indians, as Uncle Wilse had insisted but as he himself had refused to believe, were savages. This realization prompts John to warn the white occupants of a river boat that the Indians are lying in ambush. And this turning against his adopted people causes John to be banished forever by the Indians.

The title for *The Light in the Forest* Richter derives from a quotation from Wordsworth that prefaces the novel:

> Shades of the prison-house begin to close
> Upon the growing Boy,
> But he beholds the light, and whence it flows,
> He sees it in his joy.

Inherent in the quotation is one of the basic themes of the novel: the restrictions that civilization imposes on the individual. This theme actually is a corollary of the larger concept of historical change that grows out of the process of "westering," as Richter employs it; and historical change, in turn, relates to Richter's theory of evolutionary progress. As True Son, John Butler (like his adopted Indian brothers) lives as free as the open air. But returned to his white parents he experiences the constraints of civilization: he wonders how human beings live in such confinement, here where the whites have "shut themselves up in prisons of gray stone and of red stone called brick, while the larger log houses" have "been covered over with smooth painted boards to give them the glittering ostentation and falseness so dear to the whites."[16] Or, again, ordered by his white mother to remove his Indian dress and wear white clothes, the boy stares "with loathing at the pants and jacket" that he considers "symbols of all the lies, thefts, and murders by the white man."[17] True Son thus affiliates himself with Worth and Wyitt Luckett of the historical trilogy, Henry Free of *The Free Man,* Tacey Cromwell of the novel of the same name, and, particularly, Stone Girl of *A Country of Strangers,* all of whom encounter restriction in some form imposed by civilization. In all their cases, the nature of the change wrought by "progress" may be questioned.

Still other corollaries of historical change set forth in *The Light in the Forest* are the themes of America as an ethnic melting pot, illustrated by the marriage of Little Crane and his white wife; the mixed allegiance of an individual to two opposing ethnic groups, represented mainly by John Butler (True Son); and the duality of civilization that is at once good and evil, shown in the contrast between John's decent white father, on the one hand, and his evil uncle Wilse, on the other. In promoting the theme of America as an ethnic melting pot, *The Light in the Forest* becomes linked with *The Free Man,* "As It Was in the Beginning," and *A Country of Strangers.* Finally, the theme of the duality of civilization links *The Light in the Forest* with *The Town, The Trees, The Sea of Grass,* stories in *Early Americana,* and *A Country of Strangers.*

The contrast between Indian and white, of course, is not simply that between good and evil. True Son at first thinks so but he ultimately and sadly learns better. The moment of truth in which he discovers his adopted Indians to be as savage as his own whites haunts the youth. True Son and Half Arrow watch other Indians take the scalps they have lifted from whites, stretch them on red hoops and trim off the uneven pieces, and then dance in victory for their coups. As he watched, however, True Son "tried to forget what he had said to his white mother, that never had he seen a child's scalp taken by his Indian people."[18] Here, then, Richter introduces into his novel the theme of appearance and reality, and thereby touches also on the ambiguity of good and evil.

While objectively treating both white and Indian, the author still reflects something of a bias for the latter. His portrayal of True Son and Cuyloga reveals the author to be sympathetic with the Noble Savage concept of early romantic literature in America. Further strengthening this impression is the fact that only two of the whites (Parson Elder and John's little brother Gordie) are depicted as having any genuine understanding of the plight of the Indian-like white boy.

In sympathizing with the Indian, Richter brings to the novel the theme of brotherhood. *The Light in the Forest* thus resembles two earlier novels, a like number of earlier short stories, and a later novel. One of its predecessors, *Tacey Cromwell,* pleads for tolerance of human frailty, with the theme reinforced by the reaction of so-called "respectable" women to a reformed prostitute. Then, two stories, "Good Neighbors" and "The Laughter of Leen," inspired by World Wars II and I, respectively, call for understanding of a nation's wartime enemies in foreign countries. *The Free Man,* written during World War II, also makes such a plea. The later novel *A Country of Strangers* is a sequel to *The Light in the Forest,* which ostensibly explores still another side of the theme of brotherhood by seeking to promote harmony between two opposing ethnic groups in the same country. But the proximity of its 1953 publishing date to the Korean War suggests that Richter may have had in mind the extension of understanding beyond national boundaries.

Indeed, in a preface to *The Light in the Forest,* Richter expresses the hope that contemporaries, desperately in need of brotherhood, will profit from the mistakes of the past. "I thought," he said, "if we understood" how the early Indians "felt toward us even then" we "might better understand the adverse view" of Americans "by some African, European, and Asian peoples today."

In the corpus of Richter's fiction, brotherhood and its larger theme of humans enduring and prevailing signify success toward evolutionary progress. But such success does not always occur. To illustrate that point, Richter admits into *The Light in the Forest* two negative corollaries: the tragedy of youthful death and the inability of eastern civilized woman to adjust to frontier life. White children massacred by Indians (and vice versa) demonstrate the first of those subthemes, which may be found also in stories from *Early Americana, The Sea of Grass, The Trees, The Free Man, The Fields, The Town,* and *A Country of Strangers.* Illustrative of the second subtheme about adjustment failure is True Son's sickly white mother, Myra Butler. She becomes linked in this wise with Lutie Brewton of *The Sea of Grass,* Jary Luckett of *The Trees,* and Miss Bartram of *The Fields* and *The Town.*

On the subconscious and mystical levels, *The Light in the Forest* promotes the theme of the mystique of the wilderness by revealing the Indians in close contact with nature and by contrasting their way of free living with the whites' constrictions. The mystique of the wilderness is a corollary of Richter's theme of the organic unity of humans and nature, which, in turn, recalls Richter's philosophical theory that all life is governed by natural laws. In revealing the theme of the mystique of the wilderness, *The Light in the Forest* becomes associated with *The Town, The Trees, The Sea of Grass,* stories in *Early Americana,* and *A Country of Strangers.*

Like those works, finally, *The Light in the Forest* deals with the mystical theme of the search for and reconciliation with the Spiritual Father. John Butler (True Son) becomes alienated from not one, but two earthly fathers, his white and his Indian. Inasmuch as the earthly father symbolizes the Spiritual, John becomes isolated inferentially from the Spiritual Father. Compounding his problem, John does not understand his mother, whose love might otherwise have been expected to provide a key to the understanding of the earthly (and Spiritual) father. In that sense, John is similar to Chancey Wheeler of *The Town* but different from Nugget Oldaker of *Tacey Cromwell* and Jud of *The Lady,* the latter two of whom find love and understanding in the actual mother or a surrogate.

A Country of Strangers

Although published thirteen years later, *A Country of Strangers* (1966) is a sequel to *The Light in the Forest.* It is dedicated to Richter's friend and publisher Alfred A. Knopf, who shared with Richter an interest in American history and human relationships. The dedication and the title alert the reader that the novel will deal with problems of human relationships resulting from ethnic differences.

A Country of Strangers continues to explore the subject of Indian captivity that Richter first considered extensively in *The Light in the Forest.* Here the captive is five-year-old Mary Stanton, daughter of a wealthy Pennsylvania landowner and assemblyman Captian Peter Stanton, who is taken from her white home near the Susquehanna River and reared by her captors, *Lenni Lenape* or Delaware Indians. Mary's story takes place from about the mid-eighteenth century forward, the same time frame as that of *The Light in the Forest.*

Adopted by Feast Maker and renamed Stone Girl, Mary Stanton grows to young womanhood in the Indian lands near the forks of the Muskingum and Tuscarawas rivers in East Central Ohio. By the time she reaches the age of fifteen years, when the story proper actually begins, she has been married to the Indian brave Espan and has become the mother of a son, Little Otter. She finds life arduous but satisfying in its close relationship with nature and virtually forgets her white ties.

When *Yengwe* (Yankee or American Colonial) soldiers discover Stone Girl and other whites in the custody of the Indians, they demand that the captives be returned to their original homes. The white captives decline to be repatriated, but the Indians, fearful that the army will destroy their homes and hunting grounds, obey the edict. At that point, Stone Girl takes Little Otter and flees northward, seeking refuge in other Indian villages. Even in those, however, the army's edict prevails. Therefore, when the priest Father LeClercq appears on the scene, Stone Girl and Little Otter move on with him to the French settlement of Fort Detroit. There, Stone Girl becomes the ward of Madame Corbusier, who renames her Claire, and remains until she learns of the death of her husband Espan, killed fighting American colonial soldiers. Acceding to Madame Corbusier's advice, Stone Girl decided to return to her white home in Pennsylvania and sets out again in the company of Father LeClercq across the Great Lakes to upstate New York and then south along the Susquehanna to Captain Stanton's plantation. (A frontispiece in the novel presents a map tracing Stone Girl's odyssey.)

When Stone Girl arrives at her father's estate, she discovers that an imposter has already laid successful claim to being Mary Stanton and that Captain Stanton has accepted the girl as his daughter. Also, Stone Girl learns that her white mother has died during the daughter's captivity. Even though Captain Stanton refuses to believe Stone Girl's story and despite his being revulsed by her Indian child, he accedes to Father LeClercq's plea to allow the woman to live there as a servant. In that role, Stone Girl suffers rebuke and mistreatment from her own younger sister Nan, a wretchedly behaved child, and from the other whites. Only Stone Girl's paternal grandmother suspects the truth, but, when she hears Stone Girl's fable about an outcast squirrel, she realizes the girl does not belong in the white world and refrains from pressing the issue.

An Indian attack on the area around the Stanton estate prepares the way for the resolution of Stone Girl's dilemma even though it produces tragic consequences. During the fighting, Stone Girl saves her sister Nan's life, but is powerless to prevent a berserk brave from killing her son Little Otter. Out of the chaos of battle, however, emerges hope. True Son (John Butler), of *The Light in the Forest*, appears and helps Stone Girl bury her son. Later, he and Stone Girl leave the Stanton plantation under cover of darkness to seek to make a new life away from civilization. Although she seems to have lived a lifetime, or rather two lifetimes (her white and her Indian), Stone Girl is only twenty years of age at the story's end.

Like *The Light in the Forest, A Country of Strangers* has its foundation in fact carefully gleaned from research by Richter, who acknowledges his major sources in a preface to his novel: Heckwelder's *Memoirs of the Indian Nations,* Brinton and Anthony's *Lenape-English Dictionary,* Donehoo's *Indian Villages in Pennsylvania,* still other published works, and interviews with authorities. The documentation lends further credence to the authenticity of the work even though the reader familiar with Richter's other historical novels would require no such assurance. Indeed, the work makes its own case for authenticity, realistically but succinctly revealing the physical and spiritual dimensions of Indian life, including their language, which often is figurative in keeping with the Indians' close relationship with nature, and vividly revealing also the whites' conviction about their own superiority and the Indians' inferiority. Nevertheless, Richter's forte here is not in painting a large canvas in the manner, say, of James Michener, but in carefully bringing into relief representative examples of the small authenticities of daily life.

Out of Stone Girl's (Mary Stanton's) arduous life first as a white captive in Indian society and then as an unsuccessful repatriate in her original home, the dominant theme of the novel emerges. It is the haunting search for identity by a wanderer lost between two worlds. The same theme informs *The Light in the Forest* in which another white captive, True Son (John Butler), is the seeker. In Stone Girl's case, however, the poignancy becomes intensified by the fact that she is a white woman who has borne a half-breed son by an Indian husband. The history of American Indian-white relationships contains no figure more pathetic or ostracized (finally by both races) than the white squaw of an Indian brave and her half-breed children.

Although ancillary to the theme of the search for identity, other thematic threads and corollaries run through *A Country of Strangers.* Most relate to the philosophical ideas Richter set forth elsewhere. For example, the march of civilization, or "westering," represented here by the waves of whites moving from established areas to the frontier, produces historical change. One is the admixture of races, in this case Mary Stanton (Stone Girl) and her Indian husband and their half-breed child, which makes America an ethnic melting pot. In turn, it also led to mixed allegiance by people (here, Stone Girl) to two opposing ethnic groups. If the result is rejection, such as Stone Girl receives both from whites and Indians, restless wandering may ensure, as the rejected one undertakes a mystical search for the earthly father (a symbol of the Spiritual Father).

Another product of historical change is the restriction civilization imposes on individuals (Indians), who had led relatively unfettered existence in a primitive state. Sometimes restrictions may be for the better, as when they tame the Indians' savage nature, but other times they are stultifying to the spirit. Such contradictions illustrate the theme of the duality of civilization at once good and evil.

In contrasting the freedom of Indian life with the constraints of white life, Richter veers into an embracing of the Noble Savage theme prominent in the works of Chateaubriand and Cooper. That concept in turn summons forth the theme of the mystique of the wilderness. Then, as if providing a counterbalance, the novel sets forth the theme of the ambiguity of good and evil: the Indian may be noble but he also is savage as when the berserk brave murders Stone Girl's son. Little Otter's murder also illustrates the theme of the tragedy of youthful death, which occurs frequently in frontier literature. Stone Girl's stoic acceptance of her child's death and indeed of her tragic life demonstrates the theme of enduring and prevailing, which, under Richter's philosophical theories, is one of the requisites for evolutionary progress.

Those themes provide yet another link between *A Country of Strangers* and *The Light in the Forest*. They also relate the novel to such other works by Richter as *The Free Man, The Lady, The Sea of Grass, The Town,* and *The Trees,* all historical novels. Finally, one other theme relates *A Country of Strangers* to *The Light in the Forest*. The two novels present fairly and faithfully the Indians' side of their engagements with the whites. In so doing, they promote the theme of brotherhood that Richter believes should inform American dealings with peoples of all races. Brotherhood, under his philosophical theory, is the highest achievement of evolutionary progress and therefore is in short supply in the world.

In authentically portraying early American Indian life, Richter becomes one of the few white writers to treat the subject objectively. Far too many earlier writers either were too prejudiced in their view of the Indian or, conversely, too romantic in their concept of the Indian's primitive life. As Granville Hicks aptly evaluated the achievement, Richter came about as "close to historical truth as fiction can."[19]

The Grandfathers

The Grandfathers (1964), Conrad Richter's first extended venture into comedy, represents still another interlude. It falls between the second and the uncompleted third volume of his autobiographical trilogy, which consists of *The Waters of Kronos* (1960) and *A Simple Honorable Man* (1962). It precedes *Over the Blue Mountain* (1967) and Richter's final novel, *The Aristocrat* (1968).

Although creating an initial impression that it serves as a repository for unused humorous anecdotes Richter had collected during his half-century of writing, *The Grandfathers* received favorable reviews. Priaisng the "simple, colloquial, and idiomatic tone that attracts and beguiles the reader," William S. Lynch concluded that the novel has not only "broad comedy," but "poignancy too, the poignancy of place and innocence."[20] To Virgilia Peterson, the "charm" of *The Grandfathers* lies in Richter's "relishing of his characters and his poker-faced presentation of them in the yarn itself."[21] Not since "the novels of Walter D. Edmonds," in the opinion of Edward Weeks, had an American "written with such color and insight about our old primitives."[22]

Set in the early twentieth century in the mountain valleys of western Maryland, isolated from the mainstream of modern life, *The Grandfathers* focuses generally on the Murdoch clan. Hercules, or "Granpap," Murdoch heads the family that includes his wife, the "Granmam" who actually rules "the roost"; his two unmarried sons, Uncle "Heb" and Uncle "Nun," who cut logs for most of the family's precarious livelihood; his two unwed daughters, "Ant" Dib and Dockey; Ant Dib's newly born twins, the boy Jess and the girl Jessie; and Dockey's four children, the teenage girl Charity ("Chariter"), her half-brother Lancelot Gerald ("Babe"), her half-brother Wellington ("Fox"), and the baby Honour ("Honey"). This ragtag assortment resides on a white oak knoll. "On one side ran the open fields of the Magills and on the other side far beyond the woods rolled the red-shell land."[23] The family's house had "shed rooms added piece by piece, and around it the pigpen, smokehouse, chicken pen, wagon shed, the stable they called the barn and a little old trolley without wheels that Granpap had got for nothing and hauled out on a wagon years ago."[24] In such a rustic setting, the Murdochs "showed right off how they felt. They could be nice if they wanted, but holding back, scowling and yelling came just as easy, and that's what they did a lot of the time."[25]

But while the story deals generally with the family as a whole, it turns specifically on Dockey's eldest child Chariter in whose idiom it is told. Chariter has heard ceaseless joking from Granpap, uncles Heb and Nun, and others about the steady parade of births in the family. Now fifteen, she is old enough to realize their irregularity, and, more crucially, to wonder who her own father is. Her curiosity about her identity intensifies, following the birth of Ant Dib's twins, when the infants' father, Chick Saylor, becomes a resident of the Murdoch household. In joining the family circle, however, Chick neglects to enter under the bonds of matrimony, but, rather, enters by virtue of a common-law arrangement with Ant Dib.

Chariter's quest for self-identity becomes the search for her father and her other grandfather. Three possibilities present themselves: (1) Morgan ("Morg") Gandy, a supposedly reformed drunk now engaged in evangelistic preaching, and his farmer-father Nobe Gandy; (2) Sip Leck, the possessor of a fast automobile, and his blacksmith father Tom Leck; and (3) the late Richard Goddem, who died in the military service of his country in Nicaragua, and his father Squire Minor Goddem. The baldheaded, lame Morg Gandy, assisted by his wife and two young sons, returns to conduct a revival in a schoolhouse near the Murdoch place. When Chariter sees Morg, "Something went over her then as she felt him close, something never felt before, as if up to now she had been a Chinese jigsaw puzzle lacking one part lost a long while, but now that missing part had been found and put in its place, and she could be whole and in one piece for the first time."[26] Heightening the impression of the young girl, whose red hair compares with the color of Morg's mustache, Morg's wife alludes to her husband's affair with Chariter's mother Dockey. The magic of the moment vanishes, however, when, in a frenzied effort to persuade Chariter to repent of her sins, Morg moves so close to the girl that she can smell his breath, "sour and foul like Granpap's when he puked up Nicodemus's white mule," and when he starts "moving his hands around on her hams."[27]

Convinced that Morg Gandy could not be her father, Chariter resumes her search. Meanwhile, Fulliam Jones, an assistant in his uncle's undertaking parlor in Earlville, proposes a common-law arrangement between himself and the girl. When Chariter refuses, Fulliam threatens, to no avail, to start courting another girl. Further intruding upon Chariter's search for self-identity is the murder of Wichita Leck, Tom's wife and Sip's mother. Tom had given Chariter her child's ring and had thus aroused her suspicion that his son Sip might be her father. But Sip is thought by many to be the murderer of his own mother with whom he has quarreled. And while the murder mystery actually remains unsolved, it is sufficient to dispel Chariter's notions that Sip might be her father and Tom her other grandfather.

When Granpap Murdoch develops an ache in his last remaining tooth, he is dispatched by Granmam to the blacksmith Tom Leck to have it pulled. The circumstances under which Tom performs the service anger Granpap, and, when Tom's barn mysteriously burns, the patient is accused of arson. This episode serves to introduce Chariter to the third possibility for her father and her other grandfather. Granpap is taken before Squire Goddem for a hearing about the fire, and is accompanied by the entire family. During the hearing Chariter meets the squire's sister, Miss Belle Goddem, and learns about the squire's dead son Richard (Dick). Before his death in the military service, Dick had frequented the Murdoch home in periods of drunkenness and had had ample opportunity to make love to Chariter's mother Dockey.

The protracted illness of Miss Belle Goddem results in Chariter's being brought into the squire's home as nurse and companion for his sister. Here Chariter finds the answer to her quest—that Dick was her father and that Squire Goddem is her other grandfather; although the discovery is something she feels, rather than a direct revelation. Following the death of Miss Belle, the girl remains temporarily with the squire, but eventually accepts Fulliam Jones's proposal of marriage. The wedding, attended by all of the Murdochs, is held in the squire's home, and is followed by the departure of the bride and bridegroom in a hearse that Fulliam has borrowed from his uncle.

The main story line, interlaced with tall tales and subsidiary episodes bordering on burlesque, causes *The Grandfathers* to veer dangerously close to farce. And in lesser hands than Richter's it would. One of the factors that mitigates against the work's degenerating into an installment of television's "Beverly Hillbillies" is its pastoral quality. As Warren Rubel correctly contends, the term *pastoral* (once associated with a special type of poetry) now applies as well to fiction; and, specifically, to an author's handling of his material and to the reader's response.[28] That is, the pastoral poet such as Frost or the fictionist such as Faulkner, by making his "Arcadia" remote, creates a world in contrast to the complex and ambiguous environment of the urban reader and thus evokes a particular response in the reader. Richter, it is true, lacks the complex vision of Frost or Faulkner, but he still is able to portray a rustic world that simplifies human conflicts and thus evokes a response in the reader.

Further redeeming the novel from farce, Richter expertly applies liberal doses of authentic folklore. He portrays the folk medicine of Tom Leck, the blacksmith who pulls Granpap's tooth, who employs "a poultice of cow dung" to cure Dusenberry's sorrel of a stone blister,[29] and also as trimming Dockey's corns and calluses "with the expert pride of a masterhand at shaving off the horny stuff of horses' and man's extremities."[30] In recreating a hell-fire-and-brimstone sermon, the author reveals a deft ear for folk speech: "You seen that blacksmith shop down across the crick, Sister, ah? You seen the coal and iron get red hot, ah? Well, let me tell you something, Sister, ah. If you think that's hot, ah. Let me tell you if you ever fell out of hell into that red hot forge, Sister, you'd shake and shiver with the cold, ah."[31] An authentic folk song Richter assigns to Uncle Nun in chopping down a tree:

> Hi don diddy and I hit him in the eye. Huf!
> Hi don diddy and I hit him on the nose. Huf!
> Hi don diddy and I hit him in the eye. Huf!
> Hi don diddy and I hit him in the nose. Huf![32]

Mores of the folk may be seen in Granmam, depicted by Richter as having regard for the "proprieties" of eating with a knife and drinking coffee from a saucer.

Viewed for its contribution toward completing Richter's depiction of his native Pennsylvania and environs, *The Grandfathers* assumes still greater significance. With *The Light in the Forest,* Richter had shown regional life in pre–Revolutionary War times. Post–Revolutionary War and late eighteenth- and mid-nineteenth-century life here he had portrayed, respectively, in his historical trilogy, *The Trees, The Fields,* and *The Town.* Late nineteenth- and early twentieth-century regional life Richter had revealed in *Always Young and Fair, The Waters of Kronos,* and *A Simple Honorable Man.* In *Brothers of No Kin,* the author had dealt with native conditions of the 1920s. *The Grandfathers,* although the exact time is never revealed, presumably is set near the mid-twentieth century, or at least fifteen years after Dick Goddem's death in Nicaragua fighting, which could have occurred as early as 1912 but more likely after 1925. Of course, this most recent novel by Richter concerns atypical mid-twentieth-century Americans. But because it is his first to deal with western Maryland, it tends even more to complement his panoramic view.

Finally, *The Grandfathers* proves meritorious in its fidelity to themes that Richter has promoted throughout his fiction. For all of its humor, the novel contains characteristic authorial seriousness. One example is an omnisciently poignant passage in which the reader learns that Ant Dib's twins will never grow up. Less "than a week before starting school, they would take spine fever, the boy first, the girl soon after, and both die within twenty four hours of each other."[33] This revelation, coupled with the early death of Dick Goddem, is in Richter's thematic tradition of the tragedy of youthful death. And it links *The Grandfathers* with Richter's collected stories *Early Americana* and his novels *The Sea of Grass, The Town, The Light in the Forest, A Country of Strangers, The Waters of Kronos,* and *A Simple Honorable Man.*

On the psychological-mystical level, *The Grandfathers,* harking back to Richter's philosophical theories, repeats the themes of the search for the Spiritual Father and for individual identity, and of altruism. All three are embodied in the thoughts and actions of Chariter, the psychic center of the novel. The themes of the search for the Father and for individual identity appear prominently in *The Sea of Grass, Tacey Cromwell, The Town, A Country of Strangers, The Waters of Kronos,* and *A Simple Honorable Man.* Altruism is a theme appearing throughout Richter's fiction.

These virtues notwithstanding, *The Grandfathers* is not without faults. Central among its shortcomings, the characters are derivative. Chariter is little more than an updated young Sayward Luckett of the historical trilogy. Her language, including the expression often employed by Sayward, "redd up" the house, is but one example of the parallel. Granpap Murdoch resembles Sayward's father, Worth Luckett; and his wife, who also has a strain of Indian blood, might pass for the older Sayward of *The Town.* Ant Dib and Dockey, both given to free love, prove reminiscent of Sayward's sister Achsa Luckett. In fact, Ant Dib is similarly "dark-complected"; although Dockey is "yaller haired" like Sayward's other sister Genny. Two other characters in *The Grandfathers* parallel ones in Richter's novel *Always Young and Fair.* Dick Goddem, like Tom Grail, dies in the military service of his country. And his aunt, Miss Belle Goddem (like Tom Grail's fiancée Lucy Markle), cherishes the dead youth's memory. Not derivative of other characters in Richter's fiction, Tom Leck may have been suggested by the author's great-great-grandfather Frederick Conrad, also a blacksmith who, like Leck's ancestors, lived in Revolutionary War times. And Squire Goddem could have been modeled somewhat after Richter's father-in-law, Gregory Achenbach, likewise a longtime magistrate.

Another weakness occasionally appears in strained efforts for humor. The name of Ant Dib's common-law husband, Chick Saylor, pointedly resembles the term, "Chick Sale," popular in the 1920s and earlier as a euphemism for an outdoor toilet. And the anecdote implying that Uncle Robby got his peg leg "sleeping off a drunk on the railroad track"[34] produces a grotesque effect.

Structurally *The Grandfathers* is also derivative, but the practice in this instance is not objectionable. In *Always Young and Fair*, for example, Richter had employed a story-within-a-story to foreshadow the fate of his heroine. In *The Grandfathers,* he utilizes a similar device—the story of a New England father's searching for his daughter's child to foreshadow Chariter's relationship with Squire Goddem. Like virtually all of Richter's novels, *The Grandfathers* is episodic.

Over the Blue Mountain

Conrad Richter's *Over the Blue Mountain* (1967) is a novelette linked as an interlude with *The Grandfathers* because of its folkloric content. Primarily intended for children, it explores Pennsylvania Dutch folk tales and superstitions, especially a legend that, as he says in a dedicatory note in the work, Richter first heard from a Mrs. Harry Dollman. But although based on the legend, the story concerns an actual experience, as Richter implies again in the dedicatory note: "To John Brommer who with John Stine went to the mountain to see Mary."

Only seventy-eight pages long, the story focuses upon two Pennsylvania Dutch *buvas* (boys), Abie Fidler and Henner Ney, who have heard the legend, which says that, if rain falls on the day the mysterious Mary goes over the Blue Mountain, rain will continue to fall forty days. Abie and Henner, each about nine years of age, reside in drought-stricken Unionshtetle. On a July day in the indeterminate "long ago," they set out to find the elusive Mary and watch her go over the mountain. Of the two boys, Henner is the more superstitious, believing in hexes and telling stories about them at the slightest provocation.

The Mary the boys actually find, of course, is not the legendary one, but a young local woman named Mary Heim. She allows the boys to help her carry a basket over the mountain to the home of her cousin Lizzie Shrum. There the boys take refuge from a rainstorm, but not until they have helped Lizzie's husband Zack harvest his hay crop and bring it to the barn. Following a night's rest, Abie and Henner return home.

Obviously of slight substance, *Over the Blue Mountain* is worthy of consideration by adult readers partly because it reminds them that

Richter maintained an early interest in children's literature. Richter contributed stories to the children's magazine *John Martin's Book* and then published his own children's journal the *Junior Magazine* before he ever wrote a novel. Here, more than fifty years after he published his first adult short story, he has returned to the juvenile genre as though coming home for a class reunion. A more important justification for the adult's reading *Over the Blue Mountain,* however, is the additional insight it provides into the superstitious nature of the Pennsylvania Dutch, who figure in several of Richter's more mature works. Every tourist recalls seeing hex signs boldly painted on barns in the region to ward off bad luck, and in this story may be found still other examples of hexes and similar types of folklore. Viewed as a folkloric work, *Over the Blue Mountain* finds a place, say, with J. Frank Dobie's *Coronado's Children* and Fred Gibson's *Hound-dog Man* and *Old Yeller.*

Chapter Seven
Spiritual Reconciliation

"As a son, grandson, nephew and grandnephew of clergymen," Conrad Richter wrote in 1957, "I've been naturally interested in spiritual ideas. My first successful story, 'Brothers of No Kin,' had such a notion behind it and now I find the spiritual theme more and more in my mind as I grow older."[1] Sixty-six years of age at the time of this statement, the author acknowledged a natural tendency of the elderly to be preoccupied with metaphysical matters. Yet the topic, as he further implied and as his fiction has amply demonstrated, was not a recent but a lifelong interest. Indeed, from the outset of his literary career but not necessarily in an orthodox fashion, Richter had espoused spiritual values: altruism, brotherhood, justice, love, peace.

Because of the "manly reserve" that had stood between him and his own father (a Lutheran minister) and for other reasons, Richter had been unable to comprehend fully either the parent or the parent's God. Such personal incomprehension, coupled with properties inherent in the materials with which he worked, had thus prompted the author to explore such fictional themes as the subconscious alienation from the earthly and Spiritual fathers and the subsequent search for reconciliation and understanding. Richter's collected stories *Early Americana* and his novels *The Sea of Grass, Tacey Cromwell, The Lady, The Town,* and *The Light in the Forest*—all had touched upon this theme. The quest for reconciliation and understanding in these earlier works, however, had been to little avail. For this reason there remained another effort to be made, and *The Waters of Kronos* (1960) and *A Simple Honorable Man* (1962)—the first two volumes of a projected autobiographical trilogy—represented such an attempt.

The Waters of Kronos

The Waters of Kronos received almost unanimous praise from reviewers. *Booklist* called it an "evocative story which may be appreciated for its symbolic meanings or simply for its recreation of the past."[2] Comparing the novel with a distinguished play, Coleman Rosenberger said, "In the whole range of American writing of which I have any knowledge, perhaps the nearest approach in quality and theme" is Thornton Wilder's *Our Town*.[3] "Richter has been writing quietly and excellently for a long time," concluded a reviewer for the *Christian Century*. "With this novel . . . his technical skill at evoking the mood of the people and time reveals the hand of a master novelist."[4] As something of a crowning accolade, the National Book Award for fiction was conferred upon Richter's work.

Characters drawn from actual life inform *The Waters of Kronos*. The narrator John Donner is Conrad Richter himself; and his father and mother, Harry and Valeria Donner, are Richter's parents, John Absalom and Charlotte Esther Henry Richter. For the Reverend Elijah Morgan, the narrator's grandfather, Richter drew on his own maternal grandfather, the Reverend Elias Strickhouser Henry; and for Peter Morgan, the narrator's uncle, he drew on his mother's brother, George Conrad Henry. The narrator's great-uncles, Howard and Timothy Morgan, respectively, are the Reverends Victor Lafayette Conrad and Frederick William Conrad, great-uncles of the author. Even Cousin Rose is modeled after the author's first cousin, Rose Forrer, who, in actual life as in the novel, operated a salon abroad.[5]

Two earlier works by Richter also had prepared the way for *The Waters of Kronos*. The novel *Always Young and Fair* (1947), which has autobiographical overtones, is laid in Pine Mills (Richter's native Pine Grove); and, although the name is changed to Unionville in the later novel, many of the impressions of setting carry over. Indeed, the post-office scene remains practically intact. Then, Markle's colliery (Lucy's father's mine in the earlier novel) is carried over here. And the first name of the narrator, whose last name is never given in *Always Young and Fair*, invites comparison with the protagonist John Donner of *The Waters of Kronos*.

Even more closely related in terms of plot and theme to *The Waters of Kronos* is Richter's "Doctor Hanray's Second Chance," which appeared in the 10 June 1950, issue of the *Saturday Evening Post*. This short story portrays a renowned scientist, Dr. Peter Hanray, who visits a cemetery on an army reservation that had once been his native town of Stone Church. There he meets himself as a child, and is escorted by the young Peter to their boyhood home. Dr. Hanray has dinner with his late father and mother, neither of whom recognize him but both of whom reassure the visitor (who is ill) that they will pray for him.

"Doctor Hanray's Second Chance" thus provides a nucleus for *The Waters of Kronos,* which likewise is an allegorical fantasy set in the present and the past. As the story opens, John Donner, a successful writer now grown old and ill, journeys from the West where he has long lived to the site of what had been his native Unionville in Pennsylvania. The pilgrimage, he tells himself, will be useless; Unionville now is covered by the waters of a huge hydroelectric dam. Yet he has been unable to withstand the "yearning for many things vanished."

The rancher [back in New Mexico] had told him that horses raised and broken around ranch headquarters nearly always returned from the open range to die. He didn't know why but he thought they wanted to be near man again. It was as if the horses had remembered man as a god, and when old age came over them they looked back in their dim horses' minds to when they had been young and strong in companionship with that god and came back in the hope that their god could help them. Was that, John Donner wondered, the unreasoning impulse deep in his own mind, driving him back to this place?[6]

Arriving at the new cemetery to which the bodies of the Unionville dead have been removed, he experiences a miracle. From the driver of a miner's wagon traveling the remains of an old road, John Donner receives a ride that takes him into the past he had known as a boy. The people and scenes are as they were in 1889; only he is different, remaining the old man he was before breaking the space-time barrier and being unable to reveal himself to family and friends. He arrives in the past the day before the funeral for his maternal grandfather, Elijah Morgan, a Lutheran minister "who had baptized eleven thousand souls, worn out twelve horses, ruled three congregations and two wives." Thus his father, with whom he has never felt spiritual kinship, brushes the old stranger aside with the request to call later. John Donner is received at the home of neither Great-Aunt Teresa nor Aunt Jess, his childhood favorites. Compelled, then, to wander through the town, he is haunted at the sight of familiar faces whose future he knows. Among those whom he knows to be destined for tragic fates, Mrs. Bambrick and eight of her children will die of tuberculosis; Helen Easterly will die a suicide; Alice Seltzer will have a child by her brother; Mrs. Griff Flail and her four children will die at the hands of their husband-father, who will then take his own life; and Cousin Vic will die of consumption at Gettysburg College.

After sleeping that night in a covered bridge, John Donner attends the funeral of his grandfather and, still unrecognized, sees himself as a boy. Failing again to see his mother and being only faintly recognized by his senile great-aunt Teresa, who mistakes him for the dead grandfather buried that day, he is taken ill into the home of his parents' neighbor, Mrs. Bonawitz. There, in a discussion with the young John Donner (himself as a boy) and in a self-searching that follows the youth's departure, he discovers the answers to two questions that have always troubled him: is he his father's son? and whose face was it that, night after night, haunted his boyhood dreams? The answer to the first, John Donner realizes gratefully, is essentially affirmative. And the answer to the second is he himself, old as he is now, the specter shape of his own mortality. Thus reconciled in his mind with his father and having fathomed the mystery of his tortured dreams, old John Donner, slowly dying, peacefully anticipates tomorrow's reunion with his mother, who has promised to visit the stranger.

In terms of technique and theme, *The Waters of Kronos* is Richter's most evocative work. Superimposing image upon image (past and present, youth and age, life and death), the author even extends the dualism into dialogue through which the characters say one thing but seem to mean another. The effect is a resonance more often associated with poetry than fiction.[7]

Richter's technique of employing the fantasy of time travel recalls the similar practice of Mark Twain and H. G. Wells. Whereas the earlier writers relied on the fourth dimensional space-time continuum, Richter utilizes a metaphysical one. He thus tends to link his work, as Dayton Kohler demonstrates, more nearly with that of Thornton Wilder and Robert Frost. In Wilder's play *Our Town,* events unfold while the reader looks on helplessly with the knowledge that much of the beautiful and good will go unrecognized until it is past all recall. Similarly, in *The Waters of Kronos,* the reader has foreknowledge of what the future holds for Richter's people. *The Waters of Kronos* also suggests Frost's "Directive" in that it conveys with the same quiet tenderness and sad wisdom the inevitableness of life: "the loneliness of being, the awkwardness of communication, the fact that life wears away to a death that is half-welcomed and half-feared, the knowledge that the waters of time wash over the years of childhood and in the end man goes back to the depths where he began."[8]

For all of its somber implications, however, *The Waters of Kronos* is not unrelieved by humor. Both easing the tension and affording realistic insight into its characters are such revelations as that Emmy Swank has one of the few bathrooms in Unionville, but she uses the outdoor privy to "save the toilet." And there are light anecdotes such as that about an encounter between John Donner's grandfather, Elijah Morgan, a Lutheran minister, and one of his parishioners:

Sunday mornings, they said, he had had a habit of looking keenly out over his Bible to see who was missing, and God help those who were not sick when he called Monday morning. There was the story of Katy Gangloff, who saw him coming and hid under the bed in the front room of her log house, telling her son what to say. When he answered the door he said dutifully that his mother was over the mountain. "I see, I see," Pa-pa [Elijah Morgan] had said dryly, looking at the pair of shoes sticking out from under the bed. "Well, next time your mother goes over the mountain, tell her to take her feet along."[9]

Thematically, the concepts of time and of individual identity appear prominently in *The Waters of Kronos*. The theme of time Richter had explored in *Always Young and Fair*, in which the heroine attempts to stop the clock, and in "Doctor Hanray's Second Chance," which, like *The Waters of Kronos*, portrays an individual who travels into the past. Dealing with the theme of individual identity had been such earlier works by Richter as *The Sea of Grass, Tacey Cromwell*, and *The Town*. Both themes also link *The Waters of Kronos*, as Kohler suggested, with the works of such diverse writers as Joyce, Proust, Wolfe, Camus, and Bellow.[10] Those writers likewise have dealt with the search for self and the exploration of consciousness: Joyce's Leopold Bloom and Stephen Dedalus wandering the streets of Dublin; Proust's narrator confronting his unrecognized self in the mirror; Eugene Gant's search for the father; Camus's Clemence in the Amsterdam bar; Bellow's Henderson shouting toward the African sky. But to those earlier discoveries by the seeker that one cannot go home again, Richter adds another dimension: one can never completely leave home.

And it is this extra dimension that signifies for Conrad Richter a near-successful conclusion to his mystical theme of the search for the earthly (and the Spiritual) father. In this connection, it is important to note the ambiguity of the title of *The Waters of Kronos*. Kronos, in one sense, means time, a topic evidently making the title appropriate.

But it also refers to the ancient god of mythology who dethroned his
father and was in turn dethroned by his son. This meaning, coupled
with Freud's theory about the Oedipus complex, suggests the son-father-
hate legend that underlies the mythical search for the Spiritual Father.
It tends to imply that, even in *The Waters of Kronos,* the quest of
Richter's characters has been unsuccessful.

Richter, however, is not Freudian; and his character John Donner
does experience what approximates a reconciliation in his mind with
his earthly father (the symbol of the Spiritual). On his sick bed, John
Donner

> remembered again how the boy [himself as a child] had looked at him
> [John Donner as an old man] when asked the identity of the frightener. So
> that was why he wouldn't reply! It was the great deception practiced by
> man on himself and his fellows, the legend of hate against the father so the
> son need not face the real and ultimate abomination, might conceal the
> actual nature of the monster who haunted the shadows of childhood, whose
> name only the soul knew and who never revealed himself before the end
> when it was found that all those disturbing things seen and felt in the
> father, which as a boy had given him an uncomprehending sense of dread
> and hostility, were only intimations of his older self to come, a self marked
> with the inescapable dissolution and decay of his youth. Even the creator of
> the hate-against-the-father legend must in his bitter later years have guessed
> the truth.[11]

In short, John Donner "had found a part of what he sought. He had
learned the identity of the frightener, that it was not his father. He
saw the father a little clearer now and that he was his son."[12] This
realization means not merely that he no longer identifies his fear with
his father, but also that he can now draw strength from a source
hitherto unavailable to him: he is, in truth, "the real and true son of
his powerful, ever-living father, the participant of his parent's blood
and patrimony."[13]

But if John Donner has taken the first step in the transition to an
understanding of the Spiritual Father by becoming reconciled with the
earthly one, he still must take the second step. And, as "for the rest
that he and other men hunted all their lives, was he never to find it?
Was it part of the great mystery, of yesterday and tomorrow, of night
and the day star, of the nameless and unspoken?"[14] This understanding
of his father's God must perforce come later after time has admitted
of John Donner's fully comprehending the meaning of the reconciliation

just effected with his earthly father. It is the subject of Richter's novel, *A Simple Honorable Man,* which immediately follows *The Waters of Kronos.*

At the conclusion of *The Waters of Kronos,* however, a tentative answer to John Donner's question may be found in his anticipation of the visit of his mother. In Richter's fiction, the mother often becomes the key to an understanding of the earthly (and hence the Spiritual) father. Here, John Donner recalls that, as a child, he "could tell anything to his mother. She was never surprised, or if she was, she didn't show it. Whatever his doubts about justice and right, about doctrine and orthodoxy, whatever shocking words or still more shocking conceptions he had heard, whatever his protests or questions, she had had them before him or had at least known about them. Her calm could lay so easily the specters in his mind."[15] Now, as an old and dying man, he could once again rely upon the source of understanding. "She had promised yesterday that he would see her 'tomorrow' and she had never told him a falsehood yet."[16]

In this promise of acquiring understanding through the mother, *The Waters of Kronos* follows in the tradition of earlier works by Richter. In "The Old Debt," *Tacey Cromwell,* and *The Lady,* in which a character enjoys rapport with an actual or a surrogate mother, the positive side of this theme is shown. But in *The Sea of Grass, The Town, The Light in the Forest,* and *A Country of Strangers,* in which no such rapport exists, the negative side obtains.

A Simple Honorable Man

Although, in the closing pages of *The Waters of Kronos,* the character John Donner has achieved some understanding of his earthly father, the reader is left to imagine what manner of man Harry Donner really was. Moreover, while he has answered affirmatively his lifelong doubts as to whether he is his father's son, he has not satisfied himself as to his relationship to his father's God. In *A Simple Honorable Man* (1962), the second volume of Conrad Richter's projected autobiographical trilogy, the character of John Donner's earthly father is filled in, and further effort is made toward additional understanding of his Spiritual Father.

Like its predecessor, *The Waters of Kronos, A Simple Honorable Man* elicited high praise from reviewers. The novelist David Dempsey called the work a "paean to goodness" and "a tender and beautiful book."[17] To *Time* magazine's critic, it bore "a sweet, refreshing smell of hay, and—considering the risk involved—surprisingly little corn."[18] Richter, insisted Frederick H. Guidry, "writes vividly of the hard life of a dedicated minister to meet a variety of human needs with spiritual resources not felt to be unlimited."[19]

Set from 1899 to about 1940 in Unionville and in other small towns in Pennsylvania, *A Simple Honorable Man* is ostensibly the story of Harry Donner, who, at the age of thirty-eight, decides to sell his store and enter the Lutheran ministry. When he is struggling with the decision, his father-in-law Elijah Morgan (himself a Lutheran minister) seeks to dissuade him; for he knows that his son-in-law will have to undergo seminary training and the frustrations of beginning ministry at an age much older than that of the ordinary seminarian. Donner's wife and three sons, whom he must continue to support during this period of preparation, would compound the problem. Before his death shortly thereafter, however, Morgan changes his mind and encourages his son-in-law. These developments, which extend over three episodes, constitute the first of five books comprising the novel. Book 1 is entitled "Man of Kronos," Kronos being the river flowing through Unionville. And, while this "book" deals with the "call" of Harry Donner, it focuses mainly on the life and work of Elijah Morgan. Book 1 functions also to reflect the aversion of young John Donner, Harry's eldest child, to the ministerial career of his maternal grandfather and to the impending career of his own father.

Book 2 as its title "Seminarian" suggests, takes up Harry Donner's training, with its joys and frustrations, at seminary in Port Oxford. The seminary, West Shore College, is Susquehanna College; Port Oxford is Selinsgrove. Book 2 also shows Harry Donner as a summer-supply pastor at North Mountain. In seminary, Harry Donner radiates joy at learning and in his associations with Mr. Schubert and Professor Barbado, bachelor teachers who frequently visit in the highly domesticated Donner home. Schubert promises to lend a unique dimension to the ministry, for which he, too, is preparing, by virtue of his fondness for chewing tobacco. Disappointment comes to Harry Donner, when his booming voice, which could range from bass to tenor, is rejected by the seminary chorus.

In Book 3, entitled "The Dark Field," Harry Donner is shown at his first full-time appointment at Mahanoy, ten miles from his former home of Unionville. Although the church is well established, the minister is not satisfied; lethargy grips the congregation. A chance call for ministerial aid for an isolated mining camp at Lost Run, however, introduces him to a potential congregation. The minister thus begins to serve two parishes in one. For six years he selflessly cares for the underprivileged, including a one-armed miner who loses his second arm in an accident and a ninety-year-old woman whose deathbed confession reveals "thoughts and things some of which he had never heard of before and which he hoped he never would again."

The Donner family's pleasantest tenure in the ministry is sketched in Book 4, "Green Pastures." Wetherill Valley is the most beautiful country Harry Donner has ever seen, a pleasant relief from the "raw Mahanoy region." Even a rift in the congregation at first fails to dim the family's enthusiasm for the Manada Hill Church to which the father comes about 1906. Again serving the countryside in addition to his own church, Harry Donner seeks to console the parents of a son hanged for murder, fends off the amorous advances of a widow, and fails in an attempt to persuade a couple to make their common-law marriage legal. Valeria Donner, watching her three sons grow to manhood, loves Wetherill Valley. Nevertheless, she finds herself wondering where her future lies. She has detected a growing restlessness in her minister-husband, and is thus prepared for his resignation. The wife, however, is disappointed when her husband declines a position as assistant pastor of an influential church in Brooklyn. Harry Donner refuses the post because he feels he cannot minister there to people who really need his services.

In the fifth and final book, entitled "The Mountain in the West," Harry Donner has moved his family to Blacksher from which he serves churches at Paint Creek and Chadd's Cove. (All of these parishes have actual-life counterparts in John Richter's ministerial career: Mahanoy and Lost Run are Tremont and Donaldson; Manada Hill is White Deer Valley; and Paint Creek and Chadd's Cove are Scalp Level.) At Paint Creek and Chadd's Cove, Harry Donner completes his active ministry, goes into semiretirement, and eventually dies about 1940 at the age of seventy-nine. Valeria Donner precedes her husband in death by nearly twenty years and is buried at Unionville in the same cemetery as her father, Elijah Morgan. She has lived long enough, though, to see her three sons marry and begin their families. John is a writer, and Gene and Tim work for corporations. When Harry Donner dies and is buried also at Unionville, he leaves a legacy of good works but nothing of a material nature. His son John ponders whether his father's life in the ministry has been worth while.

The title *A Simple Honorable Man* Conrad Richter has taken from
James Joyce, who, in a letter, wrote, "I have enormous belief in the
power of a simple honorable soul." Its reference, of course, is to Harry
Donner, the principal subject of the novel. But the story is also that
of his wife, Valeria, their three sons (especially John, the psychic center
not only of this work but also of its predecessor *The Waters of Kronos*),
and her father, Elijah Morgan. Each, as previously shown, has a real-
life counterpart in Richter's family. Even in the passing reference to
"old Mrs. Christ," the novel resorts to the use of actual-life persons.
Dr. Jacob Christ was the first resident physician in Pine Grove (Unionville
of the novel), and he was succeeded by his son Dr. Levi M. Christ.
Nearly all of these characters appear in *The Waters of Kronos*. Linking
A Simple Honorable Man with *Always Young and Fair* is the character
Georgia, inspired by Richter's cousin Miss Augusta R. Filbert, of Pine
Grove, whose house provided background for the earlier novel.

On one level, *A Simple Honorable Man* graphically fills in the character
of the Reverend Harry Donner, revealing him to be truly spiritual—a
man with faults, yes, but one who achieves a large measure of God's
grace. Following Saint Paul's lead, he refuses to preach "the ministry
of ease" and spends a lifetime serving needy mountain people. "For
the [Christmas] season and an indeterminate time thereafter," he decides,
"the son of man rather than the prince of heaven would be his patron,
the man of sorrows his intercessor."[20] His decision often proves to be
a bitter one, especially when it brings him into contact with suffering
and death. One of the sufferers whom Harry Donner encounters is a
little boy: "'Am I going to die, Reverend?' he called out piteously
and fell back. The words were to haunt Harry Donner as long as he
lived."[21] Not all is sober, however. In the seminary, for example, Harry
Donner learns of a prank his colleagues had played on the president:

The other evening he [President Lang] heard a noise in the henhouse and
when he went out and counted, three were gone. He talked it over with
Mrs. Lang, and then went straight to Augsburg Concordia Hall and made
the rounds till he heard a festive air and commotion from one of the rooms,
also a suspicious odor in the hall. He knocked. "Who's there?" somebody
called. "It's Dr. Lang. Open the door." But nobody opened it. "Go away,"
they told him. "Nobody can come in here. We got the smallpox." Dr. Lang
went home and sighed to Mrs. Lang. "I'm afraid," he said, "our chickens
have entered the ministry."[22]

Moreover, the minister's work is never done. Even in retirement, as
he tells his son John, Harry Donner is "not on the shelf. I supply

Chadd's Cove twice a month. You know Hadley at Paint won't go all the way down there every week. That isn't the only place. I supply all over Somerset and Cambria counties. I help out once in a while for Nicely at Johnstown. Then there's certain sick people around here and the Cove that ask for me all the time. I have to go to see them no matter what Hadley thinks. They like me to pray and sing for them. Not every pastor can sing."[23]

Harry Donner's reward instead of a bank balance is the satisfaction of service to his God and his God's people. "I think my belief in God personally supports me," he says, "and that His presence and angels go with me, gives me grace to do what I'm called on to do and peace of mind while I'm doing it."[24] To him the letter killeth: a common-law marriage is more blessed than the orthodox one that fails; the prayer for a dying Catholic is just as essential as that for a Lutheran; no demand, not even that to persuade an enraged murderer to surrender his gun, is too great. Like Chaucer's parson he is a simple, honorable man of the church—poor, but rich in thought and work; patient; blithe; and always ready to give even in cases of doubt. He need not flee the Hound of Heaven down the corridors of time: they have always been friends.

In the life and works of the Reverend Harry Donner, Conrad Richter's theme of altruism reaches its highest point of development. Recall that altruism is represented in the author's theory of evolutionary progress. Like the heroine in *Always Young and Fair* and men characters in "Brothers of No Kin" and "How Tuck Went Home," Harry Donner administers to the dying. But like the heroines of "The Laughter of Leen," *Tacey Cromwell*, and *The Lady*, as well as the hero of "Good Neighbors," he also serves the living. Few figures in fiction thus present such a solid front of simple goodness and do it in such a convincing manner.

A Simple Honorable Man, through Harry Donner and Elijah Morgan (both long-lived), builds in part on a theory Richter advances in *The Mountain on the Desert*. In that philosophical novel, the author insists that preaching stirs up "energy flow" and floods "the circuits . . . supplying energy-deficient parts of the body and nervous system" and causes longevity.[25]

The novel also provides additional insight into Valeria Donner, the wife and daughter of ministers, and her family. She admits to herself that she has not entered wholeheartedly into the ministerial world, a reservation she shares with Hanna Schmursdorf, also the wife of a

minister, in Richter's short story. "The Old Debt." Even darker doubts
cloud the mind of Valeria Donner's eldest son, John. Religion can be
a heavy burden for the young, and John Donner finds it oppressive,
"his ear assailed by the peculiarly dry and sterile vulgate of the church,
his young life faced by the stern presence of rituals and sacraments, of
vows and austerities, of obligations and constraints, all under the
overhanging shadow of the cross."[26] In a rebellious moment, the youth
confronts his father with the question of how the minister can be certain
of the truths of his beliefs, and Harry Donner replies:

"Let's say that what you and your wise men say is really true—that all I
believe in isn't true, that the Bible and Lord Jesus, God forbid, aren't true;
that going around preaching the Gospel and salvation and trying to do good
like him aren't true. Well, in that case, when I'd die, I'd never find out it
wasn't true and neither would you. So your belief doesn't give you any
benefit there. Now let's take it while we live. Which way do you suppose
I'd be the happiest and healthiest and get the most out of life for myself
and those I try to do things for, going around practicing my belief and
believing it true, even though it's false, or believing it false and going around
believing it false, even though such a belief according to you would be true?"
    The boy couldn't answer that one. It troubled him. He had always believed
that truth was truth and best for you even if it killed you. Now he wondered
if there was more than one truth about the same thing, one truth that hurt
you and one that blessed.[27]

But Richter leaves the question in suspension. If Harry Donner
appears to carry the day in the earlier encounter, he likewise seems to
lose in the final one. Meditating on the life of his father who has just
died, John Donner, in the novel's final paragraph, "looked through the
open door to the green truck and greener world outside. He thought,
all this improvidence of praise for God and good will toward men,
lavished, wasted, on an obscure log church in an obscure mountain
valley, poured out through the open door on stony fields, worn rail
fences and a poor yellow dirt road that led to the small weathered
barns and smaller unpainted houses of obscure unremarkable men."[28]
Because Richter is only mildly ironic and by implication commends
the minister's efforts, the final note could be construed as being intentionally false—as calculated to make the reader refute the suggestion
of a wasted life. Such an impression, however, is more likely to be
drawn by the reader unfamiliar with the corpus of Richter's works.
Viewed from the perspective of the author's preoccupation with the

theme of the search for the Spiritual Father, the concluding passage of *A Simple Honorable Man* suggests that John Donner still searches for the answer to the ageless question of humans' relationship to God. It is a question that occurred as early as Richter's short story "Early Americana" and continued in *The Sea of Grass, Tacey Cromwell, The Lady, The Town, The Light in the Forest,* and *The Waters of Kronos.*

The deceptive simplicity of the theme focuses attention on the general artistry of the novel. Scenes are rendered with authority, having been drawn from the author's storehouse of actual experience. The narrative is ordered with such economy that the reader finds it difficult to believe that so many details of numerous lives have been distilled into comparatively small space. Characters speak in an idiom indigenous to time and place, employing such expressions peculiar to the Pennsylvania Dutch as "Gut in Himmel" and "Dang your old liver pin."

Unlike Richter's historical trilogy, which unfolds chronologically, the uncompleted autobiographical trilogy unfolds more nearly psychologically. *The Waters of Kronos* portrays the protagonist John Donner late in life, when, ill and depressed, he participates in a miraculous return for a few days to his childhood home. Picking up at that point, but foregoing the technique of fantasy for realistic and continuous development, *A Simple Honorable Man* (though focusing directly on the father Harry Donner) carries the son John from about his tenth year to his fiftieth. Thus, together, the first two volumes virtually spanned the lifetime of the character serving as the psychic center. Had Richter completed the third novel before his death, no doubt, he would have dealt with the unresolved matter of John Donner's reconciliation with the Spiritual Father. *A Simple Honorable Man* suggests that John Donner would have found a way to be reunited.

Chapter Eight
Conclusion

Conrad Richter's America experienced dramatic change during his life-time. As its population soared from 63 million to past 150 million and upward toward 200 million, the nation became the strongest industrial power in the world and achieved its highest standard of living. The solidity of its political system was demonstrated in the crucible of five actual wars and one cold one. The American people showed a propensity for an ambiguous mixture of materialism and idealism represented by prodigious consumption and production on the one hand and by responsiveness to humanitarian impulses on the other. They also became increasingly confused, insecure, and anxious under the burden of world leadership thrust suddenly upon them in the wake of World War I.

Modern confusion resulted partly from the American ambivalence toward materialism and idealism, which precluded the development of a dominant social philosophy in America. In turn, the absence of such a central belief carried over to national letters. It was reflected in a homogeneous blend of literature at once obscure and esoteric, on the one hand, and simple, on the other—the product of an uncommon number of conflicting movements. From that multiplicity of literary fashions, however, two general trends emerged. One was the realistic-naturalistic movement carried over from nineteenth-century Europe but with the additional dimension of a symbolic or mythic quality that elevated it above mere documentation. The other was the psychological tradition.

Amid those drifts of national life and letters, Richter wrote quietly and effectively for nearly sixty years. The products of his labors numbered fifteen novels, a novelette, two collections of short stories, more than fifty uncollected ones, two book-length essays, and several articles. Some of those revealed Richter to have attuned himself to modern problems and literary fashions, but others, including his best efforts, showed him to have avoided both. Nevertheless, in turning from the present to the past for fictional materials, Richter consistently focused on human qualities that he considered fundamental for a successful adaptation to modern complexity. Then, if he defied classification either as a naturalistic-realistic or as a psychological writer, he embraced characteristics of all.

Richter was one of America's most autobiographical writers. Whether he wrote of his own time or of the past, he drew largely on personal experience—either that of himself or of his family and other persons he had known. But for his historical fiction he added to the materials obtained from those oral sources information gleaned from old documents, letters, newspapers. The use of the familiar, of course, is not inherently meritorious. To the contrary, it can result, as occasionally it does for Richter, in a tendency toward sentimentality. Moreover, it can lead, as it does not for Richter, toward didacticism. The real significance of Richter's dependence on the familiar is that it inclined him toward an introspection that caused his works to veer more often than generally recognized toward the mystical and mythical.

Of course, the indulgence in mysticism and myth, especially for the mere sake of esotericism, fails to distinguish a writer. What does merit acclaim is the successful attempt to utilize mysticism and myth to find new forms for the novel and new concepts about people and history. But to suggest that Richter succeeded would be to misrepresent his accomplishment. The mysticism and myth with which he worked were not new but conventional: the alienation from the earthly and Spiritual fathers and the subsequent search for reconciliation, and the assumption of guilt; and the myths of the making of the American racial unconscious; and time and individual identity. Therefore, they do not contribute to novelistic or philosophical innovation. Neither, however, do the mythical and mystical elements in Richter's fiction reflect a purely esoteric purpose. They are organic parts of a whole. The suspension thus created may be praised for the simple reason that it represents a successful attempt to elevate fiction above the level of mere popularization. In other words, Richter's use of mysticism and myth, while failing to reach bold new heights, at least places his fiction above that which never makes the effort.

Apart from growing naturally out of the fictional materials with which he worked, Richter's mystical and mythical themes—as well as those that pertain to the level of conscious action—stem from the authorial intention for his fiction to be undertones of the philosophy he articulated in two book-length essays and a novel. Those theories have physiological, psychological, and spiritual implications. The philosophical writings, however, fail intellectually and artistically. Intellectually, they defy demonstration either by scientific or metaphysical procedure. Artistically, they suffer from adumbration not by analogy, but by stated proposition couched in terminology borrowed from science but employed in a sense that science does not recognize; or, if expressed by analogy, from the attempt to identify analogy with proposition.

The failure of the philosophical foundations of his fiction might logically be expected to result in a corresponding deficiency in Richter's fiction itself. Such, however, is not so, at least in the better examples. Richter's artistic virtuosity as a fictive writer enables several of his novels and stories to transcend the limitations of the philosophical theories upon which they are predicated and to rank among the better examples of historical fiction in national letters.

Technically, Richter's artistry is perhaps first evident in concision of presentation. Most of his long fiction, which averaged fewer than two hundred pages, derived from the novella. In such a determinably short form of single effect, space and time are crucial. The author must forego the leisurely and chronological presentation of events to concentrate on central situations in the lives of the major characters. To satisfy that requirement, Richter often employed the middle-distance point of view, with a narrator sufficiently related to the principal characters to be aware of significant events but detached enough to be objective. The result, in every instance except *Tacey Cromwell,* is the appropriate motivation of character and the adequate portrayal of event.

The deft portrayal of several characters likewise attests to Richter's artistry. Sayward Luckett Wheeler, of the historical trilogy, stands as the author's finest characterization, although Harry Donner, of *The Waters of Kronos* and of *A Simple Honorable Man,* remains in close contention. Both are depicted as strong characters, but realistically, with human failings. They epitomize elemental virtue without presenting stuffy images. If their portrayals fail in any manner, it is because of their lack of complexity. Yet that deficiency is somewhat calculated: Sayward is essentially simple in order to form a complementary contrast with the complexity of her husband, Portius, and her youngest child, Chancey; and Harry Donner is basically unquestioning in his religious convictions not only to underscore the troubled thoughts of his eldest son, John, but to reinforce the ideas of simple goodness around which his story turns. As a portrait of pioneer woman, Sayward Luckett Wheeler is without peer in American literature. As a representation of the minister, Harry Donner is almost as well established, although less complex but more virtuous, than (and hence as memorable as) Arthur

Dimmesdale, and more realistic and less didactic than Harold Bell Wright's shepherd of the hills.

Inferior in characterization only to Sayward and Harry, Jim and Lutie Brewton stand out in the gallery of western fictional portraits. In the husband are instilled the same pioneer virtues of Sayward; in him, too, is imbued a similar lack of complexity. Jim Brewton's deficiency, unlike that of Sayward, does not admit a complementary contrast into *The Sea of Grass,* and for that reason is a weakness of portrayal. Yet, in so delineating his archetypal rancher, Richter probably was making a concession to reality. The man who conquered hostile men and nature to carve out a southwestern cattle ranch in real life often lacked complexity or at least the ability to articulate his philosophical speculations. Furthermore, a cattleman's reflections about the ambiguity of good and evil seldom deterred violence in a violent land. Withal, Jim Brewton's lack of complexity is not nearly so pronounced as that of the stereotyped rancher; and for that reason he stands actually between Walter Van Tilburg Clark's idealistic Arthur Bridges and his pragmatic brother Curt. Western fiction has produced few men characters any more memorable. Likewise, Lutie Brewton is a memorable ranch woman but not because she represents the qualities usually associated with the type. Rather, she is an exception, a woman who refuses to surrender her femininity and to compromise beauty and grace in a land anything but conducive to the preservation of such qualities. Her limited success projects her above the heroine in Dorothy Scarborough's *The Wind,* in which the delicate woman fails completely. It further creates the impression that Lutie is less a pawn of fate than any of Hamlin Garland's pioneer women.

A simplicity of style, occasionally becoming lyrical, enabled Richter to create evocative settings. Then, that style also served Richter well in transmitting idiom into dialogue and folkloric materials into the dramatic framework of a work. In sum, his style enhanced Richter's envious ability to depict the actualities of a place and time. With respect to Richter's ability to present dialogue, it should be noted that few writers have Richter's talent or, in Robert Penn Warren's apt phrase, "true ear" for indigenous speech. Elizabeth Madox Roberts and George W. Harris before Richter had such a talent; and Eudora Welty, Caroline Gordon, Erskine Caldwell, and William Faulkner—contemporary with Richter—had it. In that technique and among that company, Richter had no peer. Such an achievement combined with Richter's successful execution of plot, characterization, and setting to enable his best works to maintain an admirable unity of effect.

Of Richter's works, *The Sea of Grass,* the historical trilogy (*The Trees, The Fields,* and *The Town*), *The Waters of Kronos,* and *A Simple Honorable Man* are highly successful novels; and *Early Americana* is a worthy collection of short stories. *The Lady,* more successful certainly than, say, *Tacey Cromwell,* nevertheless is inferior to those six novels. Decidedly minor works are Richter's first collection of short stories, *Brothers of No Kin and Other Stories,* and the novels *The Free Man, Always Young and Fair, The Light in the Forest, The Grandfathers, A Country of Strangers, The Mountain on the Desert,* and *The Aristocrat.* The novelette *Over the Blue Mountain* is a well-turned juvenile.

Richter's chief contribution is in historical fiction. His historical works reflect an understanding of early life, a feeling for history, and a knack for deftly expressing such understanding and feeling. No careful history of American fiction in the twentieth century, as Granville Hicks once said, could ignore Richter's work. Of course, the limitations of historical fiction become the limitations of the historical writer. For that reason, finally, Richter falls slightly short of the front ranks of American novelists: Hawthorne, Melville, Twain, James, Hemingway, and Faulkner.

Yet his limitations do not deprive Richter of a place among the foremost American historical novelists. If Cooper portrayed the epic frontier hero in Leatherstocking, Richter provided the model pioneer heroine in Sayward Luckett Wheeler. If Willa Cather enshrined the midwestern landscape, Richter sanctified the southwestern sea of grass and the eastern sea of trees. If Elizabeth Madox Roberts preserved the idiom of her Kentucky South, Richter conserved the dialect of his Pennsylvania Dutch. If Thomas Wolfe showed that one could not return home again, Richter revealed the opposite truth that one could never quite leave it. And if any writer effectively elevated complex human achievement, Richter promoted with artistic restraint the worth of simple goodness.

Notes and References

Chapter One

1. Unless otherwise noted, biographical details in this book are from author's interviews 23–24 August 1962 with Conrad Richter.

2. For biographical details on Elias S. Henry, Frederick W. Conrad, Victor L. Conrad, George C. Henry, and John A. Richter, I am indebted to G. Elson Ruff, "An Honest Novel of the Parsonage," *Lutheran* 44 (30 May 1962):14–20, and to Ruff's assistance in providing by letter additional information.

3. "That Early American Quality," *Atlantic Monthly,* September 1950, 28.

4. "Far Away and Long Ago," broadcast manuscript, 1956, 3.

5. *A Simple Honorable Man* (New York: Alfred A. Knopf, 1962), 4–5.

6. "That Early American Quality," 29.

7. Ibid., 28.

8. Ibid.

9. *Simple Honorable Man,* 44.

10. Ruff, "An Honest Novel," 19.

11. Ibid., 18–19.

12. "My great-aunt Esther Conrad," Richter recalled in our interview, "had told me about the Indians; about her namesake, queen of the Senecas." Those stories whetted the young Richter's desire for adventure.

13. "Far Away and Long Ago," 2.

14. Richter drew upon his experiences as a farm laborer for such short stories as "Suicide," "Smokehouse," and "Cabbages and Shoes," as well as the novel *The Fields;* as a bank clerk, "Bad Luck is Good Luck," "The Sure Thing," and *Tacey Cromwell;* and as a timberman, "Forest Mould" and "Tempered Copper."

15. This quotation is from written statements Richter provided during author's interviews 23–24 August 1962.

16. Edward J. O'Brien included "Brothers of No Kin" in his edition of *The Best Short Stories of 1915* (Boston: Small, Maynard, 1915), and Richter selected it as the title piece of his first collected volume *Brothers of No Kin and Other Stories.*

17. *Twentieth Century Authors,* edited by Stanley Kunitz and Howard Haycraft (New York: Wilson, 1942), 1172.

18. Ibid.

19. "Far Away and Long Ago," 3.

20. Letter, 5 November 1962, from Richter to author.
21. "Pennsylvania," *Holiday,* October 1955, 100.
22. Ibid., 99.
23. Ibid., 112.
24. *The Waters of Kronos* (New York: Alfred A. Knopf, 1960), 4.
25. "Valley from the Past," *Country Beautiful,* April 1963, 9.
26. Ibid., 13.
27. *The Mountain on the Desert* (New York: Alfred A. Knopf, 1955), 232.
28. "Three Towns I Love," *Holiday,* December 1953, 55.
29. Walter S. Campbell, *The Book Lover's Southwest* (Norman: University of Oklahoma Press, 1955), 19.

Chapter Two

1. Bruce Sutherland and Frederic I. Carpenter, in otherwise notable articles, err in attributing three early book-length essays to Richter. Both mistakenly identify the subtitle "Life Energy" as a nonexistent third volume. See Bruce Sutherland, "Conrad Richter's Americana," *New Mexico Quarterly* 15 (Winter 1945):413–22; and Frederic I. Carpenter, "Conrad Richter's Pioneers: Reality and Myth," *College English* 12 (November 1950):77–84.
2. *Mountain on the Desert,* 13.
3. *Human Vibration* (New York: Dodd, Mead, 1926), 30.
4. Ibid., 33.
5. Ibid., 40.
6. Ibid., 41.
7. Ibid., 60–61.
8. Ibid., 87.
9. Ibid., 52.
10. Ibid., 96.
11. Ibid., 22.
12. This quotation is from written statements Richter provided during author's interviews 23–24 August 1962.
13. *Principles in Bio-Physics* (Harrisburg, Pa.: Good Books Co., 1927), 10.
14. Ibid., 12.
15. Ibid., 13.
16. Ibid., 16.
17. Ibid., 16–17.
18. Ibid., 37.
19. *Mountain on the Desert,* 53.
20. Harvena Richter, the novelist's daughter, told me that the character Michael "was taken from a friend of my father's in the Sandia Mountains to expound certain theories, some of which were my father's. He was a

Russian whose first name was Henry. That the name Michael is also my father's middle name was coincidental."

21. *Mountain on the Desert,* 16.

22. Ibid., 23.

23. Ibid., 20.

24. Ibid., 29.

25. Ibid., 12.

26. Ibid., 30.

27. *Human Vibration,* 16.

28. *Principles in Bio-Physics,* 10.

29. Joseph Wood Krutch, review of *The Mountain on the Desert, New York Times Book Review,* 5 June 1955, 18.

30. Carpenter, "Conrad Richter's Pioneers," 78.

31. *Booklist* 51 (1 July 1955):447.

32. Sutherland, "Conrad Richter's Americana," 416.

33. Malcolm Cowley, "The Unsettled Literary Future of the U.S.," *Saturday Review,* 9 June 1962, 15.

34. This quotation is from written statements Richter provided during author's interviews 23–24 August 1962.

35. Ibid.

36. Ibid.

37. "Far Away and Long Ago," 3.

38. Richter, headnote to an excerpt from *The Sea of Grass* in *This is My Best,* edited by Whit Burnett (New York: Dial Press, 1942), 415.

39. This quotation is from written statements Richter provided during author's interviews 23–24 August 1962.

40. *Mountain on the Desert,* 68.

41. This quotation is from written statements Richter provided during author's interviews 23–24 August 1962.

42. *Mountain on the Desert,* 69.

43. Ibid., 70.

44. This quotation is from written statements Richter provided during author's interviews 23–24 August 1962.

45. As quoted by F. O. Mathiessen, *American Renaissance* (New York: Oxford University Press, 1941), 134.

46. "Far Away and Long Ago," 4.

47. This quotation is from written statements Richter provided during author's interviews 23–24 August 1962.

48. "Far Away and Long Ago," 4.

Chapter Three

1. *Brothers of No Kin and Other Stories* (New York: Hinds, Hayden & Eldredge, 1924), 11–12.

2. Ibid., 31–32.

3. *Human Vibration*, 53.

4. Ibid., 192.

5. This quotation is from an inscription by Richter in author's personal copy of *Brothers of No Kin*.

6. This quotation is from written statements Richter provided during author's interviews 23–24 August 1962.

7. *Brothers of No Kin*, 264.

8. Ibid., 249.

Chapter Four

1. "New Mexico Was Our Fate," *New Mexico Magazine*, March 1957, 20.

2. *Early Americana* (New York: Alfred A. Knopf, 1936), v.

3. Letter, 4 July 1962, from T. M. Pearce to author.

4. "New Mexico Was Our Fate," 21.

5. Ibid., 45.

6. Ibid.

7. Ibid.

8. Sutherland, "Conrad Richter's Americana," 413.

9. Ibid., 417.

10. See n. 1, Chap. 1.

11. Charles J. Finger, "The Old Southwest," *Saturday Review*, 8 August 1936, 7.

12. Stanley Young, review of *Early Americana*, *New York Times Book Review*, 2 August 1936, 7.

13. John T. Flanagan, "Conrad Richter: Romancer of the Southwest," *Southwest Review* 43 (Summer 1958):191.

14. *Early Americana*, 13.

15. Ibid., 20.

16. Ibid., 8–9.

17. D. H. Lawrence, *Studies in Classic American Literature* (New York: Doubleday, 1953), 16–17.

18. *Early Americana*, 3–4.

19. Ibid., 140.

20. "Southwest Pageant," *Saturday Review*, 27 February 1937, 10. Representative of the praise heaped upon *The Sea of Grass* are Michael Sayers's estimate (*Nation*, 27 February 1937, 247) that the work is "an excellent example of the novella"; Stanley Young's citation (*New York Times Book Review*, 21 February 1937, 16) of the novelist's ability "to evoke atmosphere"; J. Frank Dobie's conclusion (*Guide to Life and Literature of the Southwest* [Dallas: Southern Methodist University Press, 1952], 182) that the novel is "a kind of prose poem, beautiful and tragic." For *The Sea of*

Grass and *The Trees* (1940), Richter received the gold medal for literature from the Society of Libraries of New York University.

21. Commenting on the financial aspects of Richter's career, his literary agent Paul Reynolds, Jr., told me in an interview 27 August 1962 that Richter would have been "more successful commercially if he could [have written] faster."

22. Five other novels by Richter also have been filmed for motion pictures and television: *Tacey Cromwell, The Light in the Forest,* and the *Awakening Land* trilogy (*The Trees, The Fields,* and *The Town*). In a 7 July 1962 letter to author, Richter said of the three films made of his novels to that point (*The Sea of Grass, Tacey Cromwell,* and *The Light in the Forest*): "I have never seen adaptations of my work with the exception of one. After resisting invitations to view *The Sea of Grass,* my wife and daughter came into the New York apartment one day and said I must now give in, that the Eighth Street Theatre had put my name up in lights above those of Katherine Hepburn and Spencer Tracy. I couldn't refuse the manager my small presence and saw most of it."

23. Unlike the motion picture version of *The Sea of Grass,* the novel never shows Colonel Brewton revealing outwardly that he considers Lutie unfaithful.

24. *The Sea of Grass,* (New York: Alfred A. Knopf, 1937), 41–42.

25. Ibid., 23–24.

26. Ibid., 5.

27. Ibid., 148.

28. Campbell, *Book Lover's Southwest,* 258.

29. Dorothea Brande Collins, "Reading at Random," *American Review* 9 (April 1937):100.

30. "Southwest Pageant," 10.

31. William DuBois, review of *Tacey Cromwell, New York Times Book Review,* 25 October 1942, 7.

32. Review of *Tacey Cromwell, Nation,* 9 January 1943, 67.

33. Review of *Tacey Cromwell, New Republic,* 7 December 1942, 802.

34. Letter, 2 July 1951, from Richter to the editor of *Current Biography.*

35. Here I am indebted to Marvin J. LaHood, *Conrad Richter's America* (The Hague and Paris: Mouton, 1975), 45–46.

36. Sutherland, "Conrad Richter's Americana," 421.

37. Flanagan, "Conrad Richter," 192.

38. *Tacey Cromwell* (New York: Alfred A. Knopf, 1942), 5.

39. Ibid., 23.

40. Oliver LaFarge, review of *The Lady, New York Times Book Review,* 19 May 1957, 5.

41. Coleman Rosenberger, "Western Drama in Conrad Richter's Novel," *New York Herald Tribune Book Review,* 19 May 1957, 6.

42. Edward Weeks, "The Peripatetic Reviewer," *Atlantic Monthly,* July 1957, 84.

43. *The Lady* (New York: Alfred A. Knopf, 1957), 75.

44. In the following comparison, I follow Flanagan, "Conrad Richter," 193 ff.

45. *The Lady,* 180.

46. Ibid., 155.

47. Ibid., 95.

48. Ibid., 191.

49. Ibid., 91.

50. Letter, 14 August 1957, from Richter to Helen Treadwell.

51. Walter Havighurst, "The Lady," *Saturday Review,* 25 May 1957, 14.

52. Dayton Kohler, "Conrad Richter: Early Americana," *College English* 8 (February 1947):221.

53. T. M. Pearce, "Conrad Richter," *New Mexico Quarterly Review,* 20 (Winter 1950):371.

Chapter Five

1. Rosamond Lehman, review of *The Trees, Spectator,* 17 May 1940, as quoted in *A Library of Literary Criticism: Modern American Literature,* edited by Dorothy Nyren (New York: Frederick Ungar, 1960), 396.

2. Richard A. Cordell, "Pioneer Family," *Saturday Review,* 2 March 1940, 5–6.

3. Rose Feld, review of *The Trees, New York Times Book Review,* 3 March 1940, 6.

4. Max Gissen, "The Forest Primeval," *New Republic,* 18 March 1940, 384.

5. Letter, 14 May 1962, from Richter to Tom Gries.

6. Edward Weeks, "The Peripatetic Reviewer," *Atlantic Monthly,* August 1950, 81.

7. As quoted by LaHood, *Conrad Richter's America,* 61.

8. Sutherland, "Conrad Richter's Americana," 419.

9. "Outstanding Books, 1931–1961," *American Scholar* 30 (Fall 1961):619–20.

10. Carpenter, "Conrad Richter's Pioneers," 80.

11. *The Trees* (New York: Alfred A. Knopf, 1940), 3.

12. Ibid., 8.

13. Ibid., 11.

14. Carpenter, "Conrad Richter's Pioneers," 79.

15. *The Trees,* 99.

16. Ibid., 94.

17. Ibid., 257.

18. Ibid., 261.

19. Ibid., 276.

20. Ibid., 83.

21. In this interpretation of ritualistic scenes, I follow LaHood, *Conrad Richter's America,* 66.

22. Theodore M. Purdy, "Life in the Early 1800's," *Saturday Review,* 13 April 1946, 72.

23. Alfred Butterfield, review of *The Fields, New York Times Book Review,* 31 March 1946, 6.

24. Carpenter, "Conrad Richter's Pioneers," 82.

25. Louis Bromfield, "Another Volume in Mr. Richter's Fine Frontier Saga," *New York Herald Tribune Book Review,* 23 April 1950, 5.

26. Walter Van Tilburg Clark, review of *The Town, New York Times Book Review,* 23 April 1950, 4.

27. Pearce, "Conrad Richter," 372.

28. Carpenter, "Conrad Richter's Pioneers," 81.

29. John T. Flanagan, "Folklore in the Novels of Conrad Richter," *Midwest Folklore* 2 (Spring 1952):7.

30. *The Town* (New York: Alfred A. Knopf, 1950), 432.

31. Ibid.

32. Here I follow Kenneth J. Barnard, "Presentation of the West in Conrad Richter's Trilogy," *Northwest Ohio Quarterly* 29 (Autumn 1957):231–32.

33. *The Town,* 235–36.

34. "That Early American Quality," 26–31.

35. Carpenter, "Conrad Richter's Pioneers," 82.

36. Ibid., 82–83.

37. *The Town,* 362.

38. Ibid., 365.

39. *The Trees,* 302.

Chapter Six

1. Ben Jones, "Pennsylvania Dutch Colony," *Saturday Review,* 11 September 1943, 10.

2. Edward Weeks, "The Peripatetic Reviewer," *Atlantic Monthly,* November 1943, 122.

3. Ibid., 122–23.

4. Cassie Meredith, "Squandered Devotion," *Saturday Review,* 12 April 1947, 26.

5. Review, of *Always Young and Fair, New Republic,* 2 April 1947, 33.

6. Rose Feld, "Psychological Triangle," *New York Herald Tribune Book Review,* 30 March 1947, 10.

7. Edward Weeks, "The Peripatetic Reviewer," *Atlantic Monthly*, April 1947, 144.

8. *Always Young and Fair* (New York: Alfred A. Knopf, 1947), 50.

9. Review of *The Aristocrat, Time*, 27 September 1968, 103–4.

10. The motion picture version of *The Light in the Forest*, unlike the novel, introduces an improbably romantic interest between the protagonist John Butler and an indentured servant girl.

11. Lewis Gannett, "Conrad Richter's Tale of the Frontier World of Indian and White," *New York Herald Tribune Book Review*, 17 May 1953, 3.

12. Review of *The Light in the Forest, Nation*, 6 June 1953, 488.

13. Edward Weeks, "The Peripatetic Reviewer," *Atlantic Monthly*, July 1953, 81.

14. Maurice D. Schamier, "Conrad Richter's *The Light in the Forest:* An Ethnohistorical Approach to Fiction," *Ethnohistory* 7 (Fall 1960):327–98.

15. Adolph W. Schalck, *History of Schuykill County* (Philadelphia: 1907), 1:293, n.

16. *The Light in the Forest* (New York: Alfred A. Knopf, 1953), 38.

17. Ibid., 55–56.

18. Ibid., 161.

19. Granville Hicks, "Caught between Two Ways of Life," *Saturday Review*, 14 May 1966, 28.

20. William S. Lynch, "From Hooch to Hearse," *Saturday Review*, 23 May 1964, 46.

21. Virgilia Peterson, review of *The Grandfathers, New York Times Book Review*, 24 May 1964, 5.

22. Edward Weeks, "the Peripatetic Reviewer," *Atlantic Monthly*, June 1964, 132.

23. *The Grandfathers* (New York: Alfred A. Knopf, 1964), 13.

24. Ibid.

25. Ibid., 9.

26. Ibid., 47.

27. Ibid., 51–52.

28. Warren Rubel, "Rustic," *Christian Century*, 1 July 1964, 863.

29. *The Grandfathers*, 33.

30. Ibid.

31. Ibid., 51.

32. Ibid., 38.

33. Ibid., 16.

34. Ibid., 57.

Chapter Seven

1. Letter, 14 August 1957, from Richter to Helen Treadwell.

2. Review of *The Waters of Kronos, Booklist* 56 (15 May 1960):570.

3. Coleman Rosenberger, "Mr. Richter's Magic Touch," *New York Herald Tribune Book Review,* 17 April 1960, 1.

4. Review of *The Waters of Kronos, Christian Century,* 5 October 1960, 1158.

5. In a 2 March 1963 letter, Richter wrote me that Rose Forrer was the daughter of Charlotte Conrad after whom Richter's mother was named. Charlotte Conrad's brother Victor Conrad died at Gettysburg College, an incident mentioned by Richter in *The Waters of Kronos.*

6. *Waters of Kronos,* 22–23.

7. Dayton Kohler, "The Waters of Kronos," *Masterplots 1961 Annual* (New York: Salem Press, 1961), 293.

8. Ibid.

9. *Waters of Kronos,* 113.

10. Kohler, "Waters of Kronos," 292.

11. *Waters of Kronos,* 161.

12. Ibid., 172.

13. Ibid., 169.

14. Ibid., 173.

15. Ibid., 83–84.

16. Ibid., 176.

17. David Dempsey, "In the Footsteps of the Nazarene," *Saturday Review,* 28 April 1962, 19.

18. Review of *A Simple Honorable Man, Time,* 27 April 1962, 88.

19. Frederick H. Guidry, "Minister in the Mining Country," *Christian Science Monitor,* 17 May 1962, C7.

20. *Simple Honorable Man,* 234.

21. Ibid., 228.

22. Ibid., 48.

23. Ibid., 285.

24. Ibid., 190.

25. *Mountain on the Desert,* 16.

26. *Simple Honorable Man,* 179.

27. Ibid., 190–91.

28. Ibid., 304.

Selected Bibliography

PRIMARY SOURCES

Collected Short Stories

Brothers of No Kin and Other Stories. New York: Hinds, Hayden, & Eldredge, 1924. Contains twelve stories previously published individually: "Brothers of No Kin," "The Old Debt," "Smokehouse," "Tempered Copper," "Bad Luck is Good Luck" (originally "You're Too Contwisted Satisfied—Jim Ted!"), "Forest Mould" (originally "The Making of 'Val' Pierce"), "The Laughter of Leen," "Over the Hill to the Rich House," "The Sure Thing," "Suicide" (originally "The Man Who Hid Himself"), "Swanson's 'Home Sweet Home,'" and "Wings of a Swallow."

Early Americana. New York: Alfred A. Knopf, 1936. Contains nine stories previously published individually: "As It Was in the Beginning," "Buckskin Vacation," "Early Americana," "Early Marriage," "Frontier Woman," "Long Drouth" (originally "Long Engagement"), "New Home," "Smoke over the Prairie," and "The Square Piano."

The Rawhide Knot and Other Stories. New York: Alfred A. Knopf, 1978. Contains eight stories. Three had been collected earlier in *Early Americana:* "As It Was in the Beginning," "Early Americana," and "Smoke over the Prairie." The other five had been published individually: "The Dower Chest," "The Flood," "The Iron Shrine," "The Rawhide Knot," and "The Simple Life."

Novels

Always Young and Fair. New York: Alfred A. Knopf, 1947. A condensed version had been serialized under the same title in the *Saturday Evening Post,* 12 October 1946.

The Aristocrat. New York: Alfred A. Knopf, 1968.

A Country of Strangers. New York: Alfred A. Knopf, 1966.

The Fields. New York: Alfred A. Knopf, 1946. Reprint. New York: Bantam Books (paperbound), 1957.

The Free Man. New York: Alfred A. Knopf, 1943. Reprint. New York: Grosset & Dunlap, 1943. A serialized version had appeared under the same title in the *Saturday Evening Post,* 15, 22, and 29 May and 5 June 1943.

The Grandfathers. New York: Alfred A. Knopf, 1964.

The Lady. New York: Alfred A. Knopf, 1957. Reprints. White Plains: *Reader's Digest Condensed Books,* 1956. New York: Bantam Books (paperbound), 1957. London: Victor Gollancz, 1957. London: Transworld Publishers Corgi Books, 1957. A serialized version had appeared under the same title in the *Saturday Evening Post,* 30 March and 6, 13, and 20 April 1957.

The Light in the Forest. New York: Alfred A. Knopf, 1953. Reprints. New York: Bantam Books (paperbound), 1953. London: Transworld Publishers Corgi Books, 1954. London: Victor Gollancz, 1954. New York: Oxford Book Co., 1956. A serialized version had appeared under the same title in the *Saturday Evening Post,* 28 March and 4, 11, and 18 April 1953.

The Mountain on the Desert. New York: Alfred A. Knopf, 1955.

Over the Blue Mountain. New York: Alfred A. Knopf, 1967.

The Sea of Grass. New York: Alfred A. Knopf, 1937. Reprints. New York: Grosset & Dunlap, 1937. New York: Pocket Books (paperbound), 1946. New York: Bantam Books, (paperbound), 1953. London: Globe, 1957. A serialized version had appeared under the same title in the *Saturday Evening Post,* 31 October and 7 and 14 November 1936.

A Simple Honorable Man. New York: Alfred A. Knopf, 1962. Reprints. New York: Fawcett, 1963. London: Victor Gollancz, 1962.

Tacey Cromwell. New York: Alfred A. Knopf, 1942. Reprints. Garden City, New York: Garden City Publishing Co., 1943. *Editors for the Armed Services,* 1943. New York: Bantam Books (paperbound), 1949.

The Town. New York: Alfred A. Knopf, 1950. Reprint. New York: Bantam Books (paperbound), 1957.

The Trees. New York: Alfred A. Knopf, 1940. Reprints. New York: Book-of-the-Month Club, 1940. New York: Bantam Books (paperbound), 1951, 1957.

The Waters of Kronos. New York: Alfred A. Knopf, 1960. Reprints. London: Victor Gollancz, 1960. New York: Bantam Books (paperbound), 1961.

Essays

Human Vibration. New York: Dodd, Mead, 1926.

Principles in Bio-Physics. Harrisburg, Pa.: Good Books Co. (paperbound), 1927.

Uncollected Articles

"New Mexico Was Our Fate." *New Mexico Magazine,* March 1957, 20–21, 45.

[Conrad Richter and others], "Outstanding Books, 1931–1961." *American Scholar* 30 (Fall 1961):620–22.

"Pennsylvania." *Holiday,* October 1955, 98–112.
"That Early American Quality." *Atlantic Monthly,* September 1950, 26–31.
"Three Towns I Love." *Holiday,* December 1953, 55–58.
"Valley From the Past." *Country Beautiful,* April 1963, 8–14.

Broadcast Manuscript

"Far Away and Long Ago." Written for Broadcast Music, 1956.

Selected Uncollected Short Stories

"Cabbages and Shoes." *Everybody's Magazine,* March 1920, 61–63.
"Derickson's Gagoo." *American Magazine,* May 1925, 20–23.
"Doctor Hanray's Second Chance." *Saturday Evening Post,* 10 June 1950, 22–23.
"Exaggerator." *American Magazine,* June 1926, 28–30.
"Good Neighbors." *Saturday Evening Post,* 30 October 1943, 12–13.
"How Tuck Went Home." *Cavalier,* 6 September 1913, 744–51.
"The Iron Lady." *Saturday Evening Post,* 13 July 1957, 20–21.
"King Was in the Kitchen." *Woman's Home Companion,* May 1932, 25–26.
"Last Man Alive." *Saturday Evening Post,* 14 August 1948, 26–27.
"Life Was Simple Then." *Saturday Evening Post,* 2 March 1940, 9–11.
"The Man Who Loved a Hound." *Elks Magazine,* December 1925, 16–17.
"The Man Who Retired." *American Magazine,* April 1926, 20–23.
"The Marriage That Couldn't Succeed." *Saturday Evening Post,* 21 June 1952, 34–35.
"Rich Relations." *American Magazine,* March 1924, 54–57.
"Sinister Journey." *Saturday Evening Post,* 26 September 1953, 36–37.
"Teddy Saves the Day." *American Magazine,* April 1924, 28–30.
"The Wall of the House of Ryland." *Illustrated Sunday Magazine,* 21 November 1915, 3–4.

SECONDARY SOURCES

Articles

Barnard, Kenneth J. "Presentation of the West in Conrad Richter's Trilogy." *Northwest Ohio Quarterly* 29 (Autumn 1957):224–34.
Carpenter, Frederic I. "Conrad Richter's Pioneers: Reality and Myth." *College English* 12 (November 1950):77–84.
Flanagan, John T. "Folklore in the Novels of Conrad Richter." *Midwest Folklore* 2 (Spring 1952):5–14.
———. "Conrad Richter: Romancer of the Southwest," *Southwest Review* 43 (Summer 1958):189–96.

Gaston, Edwin W., Jr. "Conrad Richter." In *A Bibliographical Guide to Midwestern Literature,* edited by Gerald Nemanic, 316–17. Iowa City: University of Iowa Press, 1981.

————. "Conrad Richter." In *Dictionary of Literary Biography, vol. 9. American Novelists, 1910–1945. Part 2: F. Scott Fitzgerald-O. E. Rolvaag,* edited by James J. Martine, 305–10. Detroit: Bruccoli Clark, Gale Research Co., 1981.

Hutchens, John K. "Conrad Richter." *New York Herald Tribune Book Review,* 30 April 1950, 3.

Kohler, Dayton. "Conrad Richter: Early Americana." *College English* 8 (February 1947):221–28.

LaHood, Marvin J. "Conrad Richter and Willa Cather: Some Similarities." *Xavier University Studies* 9 (Spring 1970):33–44.

————. "*The Light in the Forest:* History as Fiction," *English Journal* 55 (March 1966):298–304.

————. "Richter's Pennsylvania Trilogy." *Susquehanna University Studies* 8 (1968):5–13.

Sutherland, Bruce. "Conrad Richter's Americana," *New Mexico Quarterly,* 15 (Winter 1945), 413–22.

Books

Barnes, Robert J. *Conrad Richter.* Southwest Writers Series. Austin, Tex.: Steck-Vaughn, 1968.

Edwards, Clifford D. *Conrad Richter's Ohio Trilogy: Its Ideas, Themes, and Relationships to Literary Tradition.* The Hague and Paris: Mouton, 1970.

Gaston, Edwin W., Jr. *Conrad Richter.* United States Authors Series, vol. 81. New York: Twayne, 1965.

LaHood, Marvin J. *Conrad Richter's America.* The Hague and Paris: Mouton, 1975.

Richter, Harvena. *Writing to Survive: The Pivate Notebooks of Conrad Richter.* Albuquerque: University of New Mexico Press, 1988.

Index